C000274807

HAUNTED
LIVERPOOL

VOLUME ONE

Published by The Bluecoat Press, Liverpool
Book design by March Graphic Design Studio, Liverpool
Cover illustration by Tim Webster
Printed by Graham & Heslip

ISBN 9781904438717

THE BLUECOAT PRESS
3 Brick Street
Liverpool L1 0BL

Telephone 0151 707 2390
Website www.bluecoatpress.co.uk

Front cover *The Lighthouse Ghoul*, page 172

Tom Slemen

Haunted Liverpool

Volume One

THE BLUECOAT PRESS

CONTENTS

How my Interest Began

My interest in ghosts started when I was a child, when my mother told me about a ghost she had seen in the mid-1970s. At the time of the sighting, we were living in a house in Myrtle Street and one night my mother was in the kitchen when she noticed a figure moving quickly towards the hall. She presumed it was my sister, but when she went to her bedroom to check, my sister was sound asleep.

Later that night, she got into bed and was about to drop off to sleep when she heard footsteps approaching. A stout woman, dressed like a Victorian maid, came through the wall carrying a platter with a cover over it. My mother said that she heard the rustle of the maid's skirts as she went by. The ghost walked straight through the bottom of the bed and then through her legs and, as the figure passed through the wall at the far corner of the room, she heard the sound of children cheering.

As soon as the figure had vanished through the wall, the cheering and the rustling sound abruptly stopped. Mum did not tell anyone about the ghostly encounter at the time, but a week later, our next door neighbour called round and told her she was moving because she had seen the ghosts of young boys standing in her bedroom, always appearing from the same point in the room, right in the corner. It was my mother's turn to reveal what she had seen, and she pointed out that directly on the other side of the wall from her neighbour, was the exact spot in her own bedroom where the ghostly maid had vanished.

Years later, I found an old map of Edge Hill and was fascinated to discover that an orphanage had once stood on the site of our old house in Victorian times and that the kitchen occupied the exact same space as the bedroom of our house and our neighbour's. My appetite had been whetted and so my interest in ghosts began ...

INTRODUCTION

In 1875, the Director of the American Patent Office sent his letter of resignation to the Secretary of the Board of Trade. His reason he gave for resigning was simple; he said he was quitting because, "There was nothing left to invent".

This false sense of security was fostered by the conviction that he was living in an age of technological marvels, which had solved all the world's problems. How wrong he was! Even today, when we compare the little that we do know with all that we do not, it becomes clear that we inhabit a world where maps and scientific theories are still incomplete; a world where people, ships and planes can still disappear without trace. There is so much on this earth that is unknown to man and only a fool, or a devoted sceptic, can fail to acknowledge this.

Many freethinkers throughout the ages have dared to confront the unknown head-on, even in the face of ridicule. In the long history of human stupidity there have been many who have steered us away from ignorance and superstition: Nicolas Copernicus (1473-1543); Galileo Galilei (1564-1642); Charles Darwin (1809-1892); Sigmund Freud (1856-1939); and Louis Pasteur (1822-1895). Each of these great innovators and their inventions were hooted and howled at in their day. Entrenched authority has always opposed new concepts, so the contents of this book that you are about to read will most definitely be dismissed and mocked by those with closed minds but, as can be seen by the aforementioned cases, the sceptics have had an abysmal track record so far!

This book is about ghosts – whatever they are. Every culture has believed in ghosts at one time or another. The

Buddhists tell us that Buddha trained himself to overcome fear by sitting in a haunted cemetery and in the *Iliad*, the Greek writer, Homer, describes the ghost of Patroclus visiting his friend Achilles in the dead of night, to plead for a quick funeral so that he might be swiftly released from the pain of his earthly ties. Spooky tales are not just a contemporary phenomenon – in fact, there are even several ghosts mentioned in the Old Testament.

In the course of a person's lifetime, the chances of encountering a ghost are surprisingly high. The statisticians say that only one person in ten has seen a ghost, but this figure is only based on the body of data acquired from people who have dared to admit that they have had a paranormal encounter.

Society's attitude to the paranormal has always been largely hypocritical. There are many people who mock the supernatural but believe, for example, that their lucky numbers will come up on the lottery one day, or who check the horoscope column of their daily newspaper to see what the stars have in store for them!

In the meantime, hardly a month goes by without news of a haunting. Many serious psychical research groups are now combating society's ignorance of the psychic by approaching universities, where they hope the paranormal will one day be recognised as a legitimate branch of science. Already, at the University of Edinburgh, a Chair of Parapsychology has been created and in London, the Koestler Foundation is an open-minded institution, dedicated to researching areas beyond the borders of what can be explained by our present scientific knowledge.

In a landmark ruling, in July 1991, the New York Supreme Court officially acknowledged the existence of ghosts, when it legally opened the way for a husband and wife to sue the former owner of the house they had bought, for the return of their $32,000 deposit. Jeffrey and Patrice Stambovsky were allegedly driven from their luxurious eighteen-room river front house in Nyack, New York, by two spectres which evidently dated from the days of the American Revolution. The five Appeal Court judges voted three to two to declare that, as a matter of law, the Stambovsky's house was haunted, overturning a ruling by the trial judge. In times to come, the Stambovsky case will no doubt be regarded as an important milestone in the annals of the paranormal.

Many of the stories within this book originated from the numerous letters and phone-calls I received at Radio City, Liverpool's independent radio station, where I used to present a regular slot about ghosts and local mysteries on the *Billy and Wally* show. The show was probably one of the most popular in the Northwest, and the response from the listening public was tremendous, confirming my suspicions that a large segment of the population is fascinated by the paranormal.

So why do scientists reject the idea of ghosts? Well it seems that most scientists think that phantoms run right against the grain of good old commonsense. When a person dies, that is the end of the story and, until someone returns from beyond the grave to take part in a repeatable controlled scientific experiment to prove survival after death, ghosts do not exist.

That is how most scientists view the subject of the paranormal but they have often had to rethink their opinions. For example, in 1803, Thomas Young carried out an experiment that showed, without a shadow of a doubt, that light is a wave of energy. But over a century later, the scientists made a disturbing discovery that light also behaves as if it were a particle. But how can a beam of light be both a wave and a particle? It goes against commonsense. The wave/particle problem is so baffling that even Albert Einstein and Stephen Hawking have failed to crack it. So, if the greatest minds of science are at a loss to explain the nature of light and gravity, how can they possibly dismiss paranormal phenomena?

THEORIES OF GHOSTS

If we accept that ghosts are real, then what are they? How can we explain them? The popular belief is that ghosts are earthbound spirits of the dead which continue to haunt a particular locality. Let us consider this interpretation. Apparently, the human brain has the capacity to store, organise and retrieve up to 15 trillion (a trillion is one million cubed) items of information, a capability that seems somewhat excessive for the ordinary requirements of everyday life. However, this complex organ was not always thought to contain a person's consciousness and identity.

Aristotle (384-322 BC), the ancient Greek philosopher and tutor to Alexander the Great, actually believed that the brain was simply a minor organ that cooled the blood. The Greek anatomist, Herophilus (330-260 BC), who was the first to systematically dissect a human body to compare it with the viscera of other animals, knew better than Aristotle and correctly recognised that the brain was the seat of intelligence. But the thinkers of the day could not accept this, opting for Aristotle's theory instead.

Approximately one thousand, nine hundred years later, Thomas Willis (1621-1673), an English physician, revived the theory that the brain contained the mind, after noting that nerves all over the body led into the skull. After taking so many years just to locate the brain, scientists then faced the daunting task of working out how the brain functioned. They are still not absolutely sure, but the brain seems to be made up of billions of intricate interconnecting nerve cells called neurons, as well as supporting cells (neuroglia). The neurons transmit electrical impulses and release chemical transmitters, which act on other neurons, as well as muscle (or effector) cells. In lay person's terms, the brain is mostly electrical in its workings and electricity is a form of energy.

According to science's immutable First Law of Thermodynamics, energy cannot be created or destroyed. So if the energy in the brain can never be destroyed, where does it go to when a person dies? Does it radiate into space like a radio wave; or does it somehow linger around, like a charge of static electricity. If this post-death electrical field was part of a person's consciousness, what would happen if it were transmitted into the developing mind of an embryo? Could a disembodied mind take over the mind of the foetus? Furthermore, could this hypothetical point explain reincarnation?

But let us not digress from our search for the spirit. Long before neurologists discovered that the brain and nervous system used electricity to function, the occultists had claimed that each person possessed a secondary body made of energy that is stowed away in the physical body. The mystics maintained that this 'etheric' body contained the ego and consciousness and could leave the physical body under certain conditions, especially when the flesh and blood body was very ill or dying. The occultists called this stowed-away entity the 'astral body', although the esoteric terminology isn't important; the Ancient Egyptians called the astral body the 'Ba' and pictured it in their wall paintings as a bird with a human face. Ancient Indian writings tell of eight siddhis (supernormal powers) that can be acquired through meditation. The sixth siddhi is the ability to fly through the sky by releasing the astral body, and there is an interesting account of astral espionage in an early nineteenth century book known as the *Bhagavata Purana*. In this amazing tome, is the story of Usha, a girl who flies out of her body during sleep to reconnoitre faraway lands and spy on friends living many miles away.

There are also Biblical references to astral travel. St Paul recounts a man he knew who, 'Whether in the body, or out of the body, God knoweth, was caught up into paradise and heard unspeakable words, which it is not lawful for a man to utter'. (2 Corinthians 12:3)

For years, the idea of an astral body was deemed to be a laughable absurdity by scientists – until the late 1970s, when a number of eminent embryologists came to the conclusion that developing limbs and organs in a human foetus are shaped by morphogenetic fields. This term means fields that give rise to form, or form-fields. The embryologists had racked their minds trying to fathom out how a human foetus changes from a fertilised egg into a fully-developed baby, after a mere three hundred and eighty days. They could see that something was supervising the highly specialised development of the various parts of the baby's body, and that supervisor was evidently not just the DNA in the baby; something else was at work.

For example, consider your arms and legs. The DNA in these limbs is identical, but they are shaped differently. Something else besides your DNA was responsible for shaping the different parts of your body and this something is still a mystery. The present theory postulates morphogenetic fields as the invisible supervisor. To exemplify this theory, imagine a piece of paper with iron filings sprinkled on it. As soon as we lift a bar magnet to the underside of the paper, without touching it, we only have to tap the paper and the scattered iron filings on top of the paper will instantly align themselves within the magnetic fields from the bar magnet and form complex shapes. Morphogenetic fields work in the same way, but they seem to be far more complex and mysterious.

Recently it was discovered that if a small electric current (0.2 micro-amperes) is passed across the stump of a frog's severed limb, most of the lost limb will regenerate and grow back. This is something of a breakthrough, because frogs do not usually regenerate lost limbs, unlike the salamander, which can regrow a lost leg in just eleven weeks. Electric currents have also been employed in a similar way to promote bone-healing in humans. All this research indicates that the human body is criss-crossed with fields of electricity and other, as yet unknown, energies. Could it be that the total sum of these energies comprise the fabled spirit body? Is that the part of us that survives the death of the physical body? If it is, could this explain the existence of ghosts?

Sceptics will say at this point that all the things we have mentioned so far are invisible; the astral body, morphogenetic fields – even the spirit. But there are so many invisible things in this world which we take for granted. The invisible electromagnetic waves in our microwave ovens that cook our meals, the television signals that are broadcast to our satellite dishes and television aerials, bringing us news, films and soap operas; the FM and AM waves that bring chat shows and music to our radios; the ultraviolet rays with which sunbeds give us a tan and even the digital signals that take our voices down the optic-fibre cables of the telephone network; all these are invisible to us, yet they are all real nevertheless.

If we take a look at the whole range of radiations known to man, we can see that our eyes can only perceive a very narrow band of radiation which contains all the colours known to us. All the colours which make up the great works of art, from Da Vinci to Dali, are contained within an extremely slender strip of the electromagnetic spectrum.

Our sense of hearing is as limited as our vision. The deepest sound we can hear has a wavelength of 22 metres and a frequency of 15 cycles per second. The shrillest sound a human adult can hear has a wavelength of 2.2 centimetres and a frequency of 15,000 cycles per second, although children can hear just above this range. Certain animals can hear shriller sounds that bypass our hearing. Bats emit squeaking sounds with ultrasonic frequencies in the range of 13,000 cycles per second and navigate by responding to the echoes of these sonar-type waves. The hearing range of the domestic dog also extends into the ultrasonic, which is why humans cannot hear the sound of a dog whistle. So, when we realise that there are radiations and sounds beyond our range of perception, we should be less doubtful about the reality of spirits.

I believe that some ghosts are spirits, while others are nothing more than images from the past that are occasionally replayed like a video-recording. Who, or what, is replaying these images of bygone days is anybody's guess. Some physical researchers think the weather may be a contributing factor; that under certain temperatures, perhaps when the earth's magnetic field is unusually intense, something happens to the very fabric of the space/time continuum, and phantoms of people long-dead walk through into our dimension. Other freethinkers believe that the mind of the person who sees the ghost is responsible. Perhaps these people have abnormalities in the parts of their brain that deal with vision; however this theory does not explain cases where two or more people have simultaneously witnessed a supernatural event.

Some people have asked me where all this delving into ghosts will lead to. In other words, what's the use of chasing spectres? I always tell them that one day, when ghosts are fully understood, we may be able to communicate with people we had long thought to be dead. Perhaps loved ones, personages of immense historical interest, or great intellectuals, such as Einstein and Plato, would be able to communicate with us once again. Mozart and Beethoven could bestow new soul-stirring symphonies to the world. The possibilities are immense. And should we discover how to induce ghostly holograms from the past through some electronic manipulation of time, the whole panorama of the past would be opened up for our inspection. History would no longer be a clutter of surmises and educated guesses, although, of course, reading about battles, plagues, inquisitions and massacres is one thing; but seeing such brutalities re-enacted before us and knowing that we cannot help those victims of violence, would be quite another. If psychical research one day reaches a stage where a technical breakthrough allows the past to be inspected, then reflect on the possibility that you, the reader of this book, could at this moment be the unwitting subject of a Primitive Psychology class somewhere in the future.

THE GHOSTLY POLICEMAN
OF SCOTTIE ROAD

In August 1971, several residents of Lawrence Gardens, near Scotland Road, spotted a man dressed in an old-fashioned policeman's uniform strolling down their street. They watched, bemused, as he jauntily swung his truncheon back and forth and used it to tap on certain doors and windows as he walked his beat. They presumed, correctly as it turned out, that the idea behind the tapping was to reassure those inside the houses that he was there on duty, ready to spring into action, should they need him.

One particularly inquisitive resident of the Gardens always made it his business to find out exactly what was going on; nothing got past him. Trying not to look conspicuous, he followed the odd-looking man up to the top of the street to get a better look at him and was struck by the fact that he was wearing a haversack with a tin helmet attached to it, like the one's people used during the war. As the policeman turned the corner of the road, the nosey parker trotted after him, at what he considered to be a safe distance, using the technique he had seen used in so many films. On turning the corner himself, however, he was stunned to discover that his quarry was nowhere to be seen. The road was completely empty – he had literally vanished into thin air!

He rushed back to tell his neighbours what he had seen and it became the hottest topic of conversation in the Gardens for the rest of that day.

Some time later, when some of the older folk living in the Scotland Road area heard of the supernatural episode, many of them recalled that there had once been just such a police constable, back in the thirties and forties. He too had had the habit of always tapping on certain doors and windows with his truncheon, as he passed on his beat. The reason he did so was to inform the elderly and infirm that all was well, because he was around looking after them, as well as to warn criminals and illegal gamblers of his presence.

At the outbreak of the Second World War, that constable, like every officer of the law at that time, was supplied with a rather inadequate-looking anti-shrapnel helmet, or 'tin-hat', as it came to be nicknamed. Many old-timers claim that the policeman was killed in an air-raid on the seventh night of the now infamous May Blitz of 1941, just minutes after rescuing a disabled child and carrying him to the safety of an air-raid shelter.

People who remembered the constable all backed up their neighbour's story and confirmed that the street near Lawrence Gardens, where the ghost was seen that day, was part of his regular beat. Perhaps, as a man obviously dedicated to his work and his neighbourhood, the policeman felt that he had been brutally pulled away from his duties far too soon, and that he still had important work to do.

THE BOY IN THE BLUE SCARF

On the wintry evening of 16 December, 1878, Doctor Charles Blunden had fallen asleep at his desk in his surgery in Myrtle Street. He had had an exhausting day's work seeing patient after patient, many of them too poor to pay him. At 7 o'clock the doctor was awakened from his slumbers by repeated banging and the incessant ringing of his front doorbell. He shook himself awake, and then, because his staff had already left his consulting rooms, he went himself to see who was at the door. Whoever it was, was in a big hurry and he groaned at the thought of having to attend another emergency, when all he wanted to do was go home to bed.

Standing shivering on the snow-covered steps in his bare feet, was a little ragged-trousered boy. The child's only defence against the bitter cold was a jaunty little blue scarf, which looked totally out of place on top of the rest of the rags covering his undernourished little body. The doctor was a compassionate man and quickly invited the poor child in from the cold, while he listened to his story. But the boy refused the offer and cried out frantically, "Please come with me, doctor! Mother's ill!"

Without bothering to ask for details of her symptoms, the doctor grabbed his coat, hat and medical bag and followed the young urchin to nearby Arrad Street, where a woman was lying prostrate in the snow. The doctor found a weak pulse, but knew that there was not a second to spare, if he were to save her life. He called a cab and took the woman to the nearest hospital, where she was treated for double pneumonia. She was gravely ill but she had two things on her side – she was relatively young and otherwise quite health – and under the doctor's watchful eye she gradually began to improve.

Some weeks later, after making a full and miraculous recovery, the woman sought out Doctor Blunden at his surgery and thanked him profusely for saving her life. The doctor was a modest man and merely shrugged his shoulders and said that it was all part of his job. In fact, it was not he who deserved the praise, but her son.

"You've got a fine lad there, my dear. Without his quick thinking, I don't think you would still be here today."

The woman looked puzzled and her lip began to quiver.

"I no longer have a son, doctor," she said, her eyes brimming with tears. "My darling boy died a few years ago … from the fever … He was the most beautiful caring child a mother could wish for … and now he's gone forever."

Doctor Blunden was speechless for a moment and then asked, "But if that is the case, then who was the child in the blue scarf who fetched me to save you that night? … He took me straight to you … and he called you 'mother'."

The woman shook her head in disbelief, then produced the one precious item of her son's clothing which she had kept as a memento, a small blue scarf – identical to the one worn by the barefooted boy. She smiled the saddest of smiles. She seemed to know that her son had saved her from beyond the grave.

THE DEADLY LOOKING-GLASS

This is an eerie story about a haunted mirror. The tale begins in the 1960s and is continuing to the present day. The mirror involved might be the one hanging in your hall or living room, for its present whereabouts is unknown.

In 1966, a Malayan sailor was found dead at a lodging house near Paradise Street. The coroner was baffled by the seaman's death, because it seemed that he had died from traumatic shock, which is a scientific way of saying that the man had been so shocked by something, that his heart had stopped beating.

What could possibly have terrified the Malayan seaman to death? The police report was intriguing; it said that the sailor had been found sitting bolt upright on a dining chair – gazing at a long rectangular mirror with a look of complete horror. His eyes were bulging and his mouth was wide open. On a stool beside the dead man, were the melted remains of a candle.

An old captain from Borneo was interviewed and said that, on many of the islands of the South China Seas, there was a dangerous ritual called 'Mirror Staring'. In this ritual, the subject sat in a darkened room, at night, with a lit candle and stared into the mirror for as long as possible until things began to happen. The person would start to see that the face reflected in the mirror was no longer his own but that of the devil within him.

The old Borneo mariner pleaded with the police, "Please break the mirror that the man was gazing into, for it contains his trapped soul. Please shatter it, or his soul will be imprisoned in it forever."

The police, of course, thought the old captain was crazy and refused to smash the mirror. Five months later, an

Australian man stayed at the lodging house and moved into the room where the Malayan sailor had met his strange death. One evening, the Australian, Phil, thought he would go into town and decided to have a shave. He was staring in the mirror on the wall, applying the creamy lather to his face with a brush, when he suddenly saw a pair of dark eyes in the reflection. He assumed at first that they were a reflection of his own eyes and that the mirror was flawed, but when he moved away from the mirror to get his razor, the eyes remained where they were. Then Phil noticed the outline of a face around the eyes and thought the ghostly reflection was that of a far Eastern man. Phil was so frightened that he ran out of the lodging house with lather still on his face.

In the foloowing weeks and months many more strange images were glimpsed in that mirror by successive lodgers. In the end, the owner of the lodging house, a thirty-year-old Irishman, bought a new mirror and gave the haunted looking-glass to a friend – without telling him of its mysterious reputation. The Irishman's friend Eric was an arty type; a poet and photographer, who was into so-called mind expanding drugs. He hung the mirror in the parlour of his house in Pilgrim Street. Over the next couple of months, several of Eric's girlfriends claimed they had seen a horrible contorted face staring out of the mirror in the parlour. Eric thought the girls had been hallucinating on LSD, until early one Sunday morning, in August 1967, when Eric learned that there was indeed something sinister and evil about the mirror in the parlour.

At 3.15am, Eric returned home from the Pyramid Club with two girls, Nicole and Sandra. He had met them both in the El Cabala coffee bar in Bold Street and had then taken them for a night out at the club. As Eric started to make a pot of coffee, Nicole commented, "Coffee? Haven't you got something stronger?"

"I'm out of pot. Hey, wait till I show you this gizmo I made," Eric replied and pointed to the record player in the corner.

On the turntable there was a cardboard cylinder and inside the cylinder was the bulb of a lamp, hanging by a wire. Eric switched the bulb on, then turned on the record player. The turntable and the cylinder rotated and the light from the bulb shone through about thirty vertical slits that had been cut into the cylinder. When Eric switched off the main light, the effect was spectacular. The light shining through the slits in the spinning cylinder pulsated, causing a stunning strobe effect.

Nicole was impressed. "Wow, that's groovy."

"It puts you in a psychedelic trance," said Eric.

Nicole and Sandra started to dance and, in the strobing light, they seemed to move in slow motion. The strobe made Eric feel dizzy but he continued making the coffee.

The girls then left the room to go the toilet, and Sandra remarked, "I hope he doesn't think we're all going to sleep in the same bed. He can sleep on the sofa."

Nicole laughed, "I think it'd be a laugh if we all slept together. You're a real prude, Sandra. Nothing will happen. Eric seems like a decent bloke."

The two girls then checked their make-up in the mirror and returned to the living room. They found Eric sitting in the chair, lost in thought. Nicole went over to him and sat on his knee but Eric did not react.

"Stop messing about, Eric!" Nicole snapped, annoyed.

Eric did not even blink, he just stared at the mirror with a puzzled look on his face.

"What's wrong with him? Is he drunk?" Sandra asked, but

Nicole realised that Eric was not drunk – he was dead.

She turned around to see what he had been looking at and saw a face that etched itself on her memory: a demonic, evil-looking man grinning at her in the mirror. She let out a scream and leapt off Eric's lap. His body slumped off the chair and landed with a thud, his lifeless eyes staring at the carpet. Sandra looked at the mirror to see what Nicole was screaming at and she, too, saw the devilish face, which had now turned to grin at her. Sandra could not scream but ran out of the flat, pushing her friend aside in blind panic.

When the police arrived, they saw the record player strobe still turning and they switched it off and turned on the living room light. Of course, Nicole and Sandra's story was conveniently dismissed as a drug-induced hallucination and Eric's death was explained away as death from natural causes.

However, the detective who examined the scene of Eric's death as a matter of police routine, happened to be the same detective who had investigated the death of the Malayan sailor the year before and he instantly recognised the mirror. He was unable to verbalise his thoughts about the haunted mirror but advised Eric's next-of-kin to dump it immediately, although he could not give his reasons for the suggestion. The mirror was subsequently given to an old lady who lived next door to Eric. Within weeks, she and her husband reported seeing not one, but two, faces staring out at them from the mirror, which now hung in their bedroom; the face of a far Eastern man and the sad face of a young long-haired Caucasian.

Speke Hall's Mystery Ghost

Speke Hall is a magnificent black and white half-timbered mansion house dating back to Shakespeare's time, which is unfortunately now almost marooned in the middle of Liverpool's John Lennon Airport. The hall was built on the site of an ancient manor house, which was so old that it was recorded in the Domesday Survey of 1086.

Since it was built, the present Speke Hall has enjoyed a rather chequered history. The original inhabitants were the Norris family but, because of serious financial problems, they were forced to allow the hall to be sold out of their family. Their purchasers were the Beauclerks, whose main residence was in the south of England. Sadly, the Beauclerks neglected their northern property; it was probably too far away for them to be bothered with, and it was allowed to fall into disrepair.

Then, in 1797, Richard Watt purchased the building, which was now in a pretty delapidated state, and set about restoring it to its former glory. Watt's successors eventually handed over Speke Hall to the National Trust in 1943 and under their careful stewardship, it has been preserved and is now regarded as one of Liverpool's greatest historic and architectural masterpieces.

Throughout the comings and goings of the various families who have resided in the hall, only one inhabitant has consistently remained, and that is the resident ghost! The phantom that walks Speke Hall is widely believed to be the ghost of Lady Beauclerk, but historians say this is highly unlikely because records clearly show that none of the Beauclerk family ever actually visited the hall, never mind lived there.

Nevertheless, the unidentified ghost has been seen by many people over the years, especially around the Tapestry Room. One guest, who stayed overnight, encountered the ghost in her bedroom, as she was getting ready for bed. It made its appearance by floating through the wall. When that section of wall was later examined, investigators were fascinated to discover a secret passageway hidden behind it. The function of this passage, which leads downwards through an outer wall, is unknown, although some believe it was a hiding hole, or escape route, for Catholic priests during the time of Oliver Cromwell.

The Cannibal Captain

This salty spine-tingler was taken from a news item in the *Liverpool Albion*, a nineteenth century newspaper ...

In July 1884, a ship named *Pierrot* capsized in the mid-Atlantic, leaving only four survivors. One of them was the captain, Edward Grace, a Liverpudlian. For three long weeks, the four survivors huddled together in the lifeboat with little food and water to sustain them.

As the days dragged on, the men grew more and more listless and despairing. Their skin was in an appalling condition from the salt and the relentless sun, from which there was no escape. Their bodies were shrunken from a combination of dehydration and starvation. Their food and water had now completely run out and if they were to do nothing, they would all be dead in a very short time. They made a pitiful sight.

It was against this background that Captain Grace decided to resort to desperate measures and hatched his diabolical plan. He used his authority as captain to force the men to draw lots, with the unlucky one amongst them to be eaten so that the others might survive. Two of the seamen were so far gone that they no longer cared whether they lived or died and agreed to the proposal without argument.

The only voice of dissent came from sixteen-year-old Richard Tomlin. Because of his youth, he had weathered the ordeal better than any of them and was still full of fight, even though he had lost a lot of body weight, like the others. He argued that he had his whole life ahead of him and didn't want to die. Surely they would be picked up soon by a passing boat.

The captain listened to his protestations in silence, then said they would discuss the matter again soon, if, in the meantime, they had not been rescued. It is one thing to eat from the corpse of already dead comrades in desperate situations such as the one they were in, but it is another matter entirely to deliberately murder one of those comrades, simply to keep oneself alive.

An hour later, reassured that he was safe, at least for the next few hours, young Richard Tomlin fell into a fitful sleep. He should not have been so trusting, because as soon as Captain Grace was sure that he was asleep, and with other two men watching, he slit his throat. Over the next four days, the three remaining men tucked into their dead shipmate's flesh, so saving their own lives. To prevent the body from decomposing and fouling up the boat, and also to preserve its edibility, the men removed rolls of bandages from the first aid box, dipped them in salt water and wrapped them round the corpse.

When the three men were eventually found, their rescuers knew at once what they had resorted to, because the boat was littered with blood and bits of human bone and flesh. They were brought to Portsmouth where all three of them were charged with murder. They were found guilty, but the Home Secretary decided to take pity on them, arguing that they had been through enough during those horrific days in the lifeboat and commuted their sentences to six month's imprisonment.

When Captain Grace had served his time in prison, the first thing he did on his release was change his name. Since the case had been widely reported, and had caused a wave of mass revulsion in the country, he was sure that no one would employ him if he kept his own name. Having done this, he headed for Liverpool to find work.

But burying the past takes more than a simple name change and one foggy night, as the captain walked along Paradise Street, he came upon the bandaged, bloodstained figure of Richard Tomlin. The terrible thing approached him holding out its hands beseechingly. Grace ran for his life but, wherever he went, the thing in bandages relentlessly followed.

Finally, in blind panic, he fled to the nearest police station and told them about Tomlin's ghost. Assuming that he was drunk, they threw him into a cell in Anfield Road Bridewell and left him there for the night to cool off.

The following morning, when they opened up his cell to give him his breakfast, they found Captain Grace lying dead in the corner. His eyes were wide open with terror and he was clutching a bloody piece of torn bandage in his hand. It seemed as if Richard Tomlin had finally had his revenge.

THE MAN IN THE IRON TUBE

On the morning of Friday 13 July 1945, a group of children were playing on a blitzed site on the corner of Fulford Street and Great Homer Street, when one of them discovered a sheet-iron tube that was partially opened at one end.

"Hey! Come and take a look at this," he cried, motioning to his mates. "What d'you think it is?"

The children all thronged round the open end of the tube but jumped back in fright as one of them looked inside and cried out when he saw something he didn't expect.

"Ugh! It's a bloomin' skeleton! Come and take a look for yourselves, if you don't believe me," he said.

The children took it in turns to peer through the opening, and sure enough, they all saw the same thing – a large adult skeleton lying inside its steel 'coffin'.

"Look!" shouted one of them. "You can see bits of its clothes sticking to it. Ugh! It's disgusting!"

This was the most exciting thing that had happened to them in a long time and after a short discussion, the eldest amongst them decided they had to report the skeleton to the police – the person could have been murdered for all they knew – and anyhow, he should be buried properly in the churchyard, just like everybody else.

The mention of the word 'skeleton' quickly brought the police to the bomb site. They carried out a brief inspection of the tube and its grisly contents and then arranged for it to be removed to the City Morgue. The children responsible for the discovery told all their friends and gathered round to watch as the tube was lifted into the police van.

"We found it, you know," said a five-year-old proudly to one of these late comers.

"Yeah, d'you think we'll get a reward, or get our names in the papers?" one of them asked the policeman.

"I shouldn't think so, love, but you can all come and join the police force when you grow up. You'll make smashing little detectives."

With that, the tube was hoisted up into the van as carefully as possible, so as not to disturb its contents. Once in the morgue a record was made of the tube's dimensions – six feet, nine inches long and eighteen inches in diameter.

When the tube was cut open with an oxyacetylene torch, it was found to contain the intact six-foot skeleton of a man and the tattered remains of his Victorian clothing. Bizarrely, the skull was resting on a brick 'pillow', wrapped in sacking. The clothes consisted of a morning coat, narrow-striped trousers and a pair of elastic-sided leather boots. On one finger bone there was a gold signet ring set with a bloodstone and bearing a London hallmark for the year 1859. In the tail pocket of the morning coat were several fragile documents which, amazingly, were still legible after all those years and related to a T C Williams and Company of Leeds Street, Liverpool.

Diaries covering the period between June 1884 and July 1885 were also found in the skeleton's coat but none of these clues threw any real light on the dead man's identity, nor did they give any hint as to how or why the body had come to be in the cylinder. It was all very strange.

In an attempt to get to the bottom of this case, I began to research the documents found in the clothes. In the year 1883, a firm of oil merchants and paint and varnish manufacturers was trading under the name of T C Williams and Company at Nos 18-20 Leeds Street, and the principal of that firm was Thomas Cregeen Williams, of Number 29 Clifton Road, Anfield.

In 1884, Thomas's business had obviously run into difficulties, because the accounts of the paint firm were being probed by a firm of accountants. Thomas Williams was apparently deeply worried about the investigations, as he knew that it was highly likely that they would ultimately lead to his ruin. It has been suggested that the poor man took refuge in the cylinder in order to hide from his creditors and probably died from asphyxiation or hypothermia. But why choose to hide in a cylinder, of all places? Surely that would be the last place anyone would choose, unless they were so demented with worry that they could no longer think straight. Most debtors in those days simply boarded a ship when bankruptcy loomed and escaped to the new world. The baffling case remains an enigma to this day.

THE HOPE STREET BODY SNATCHERS

In October 1826, a gruesome event occurred in Liverpool, which sent shockwaves of disgust all over the country. It all began when three large casks labelled, 'Bitter Salts', were loaded on to a ship, the *Latona*, which was berthed at George's Dock Passage, preparing to sail for Leith, in Scotland.

Just hours after the casks had been safely stowed in the *Latona's* hold, they began to give off the foulest of smells: the unmistakable odour of decomposing flesh. The smell was so strong and so utterly abhorrent, that it was churning the stomachs of the entire crew, and so the captain thought he had better order his men to prise open one of the casks, before he had a mutiny on his hands.

Nobody on that ship was prepared for what was about to be revealed in that hold. As the lid was prised off the first of the casks, an overpowering stench assailed the nostrils of those present, making them retch and dash for the ship's rail. The captain too felt sick to the stomach from the putrid smell, but deciding that he must show leadership, he steeled himself and took a quick peek inside. There, packed in salt and crammed together like so many sardines in a tin, was a tangle of rotting flesh, which turned out to be the remains of several human bodies. Each of the other two casks held the same gruesome cargo, and a total of eleven bodies were eventually found in the three casks.

All plans for sailing on the next high tide were shelved for the time being and the police were urgently summoned to the ship. They had no difficulty in tracing the man who had carted the casks to the *Latona* and he was soon brought in for questioning. It soon became obvious that he had had nothing to do with the dirty deeds and was only too willing to help the police in tracking down the villain, or villains, responsible. He told them how a tall gentleman, dressed in black, and with a strong Scottish accent, had given him two shillings to take the cargo of corpses to the ship, from a cellar at Number 8 Hope Street.

When the police arrived at the house, the owner, a Reverend James McGowan, told them that he had recently rented the cellar to a Mr Henderson, a Scot from Greenock, who, he had been led to believe, was in the business of exporting fish oil. The police then asked the vicar for the cellar key and when he pretended that he did not have it, they used a crowbar to gain entry, despite the reverend's threats from the top of the cellar steps, that he would be taking of legal action for unlawful entry and criminal damage.

As the police descended those cellar steps, the familiar sweet sickly smell of rotting human flesh assailed their nostrils once again. Nevertheless, they persevered, and soon the cellar door was forced open. Nothing – not even the grisly casks onboard the *Latona* – could have prepared them for what they were about to find in that dreadful place. In the half darkness, their torches lit on a scene of utter carnage, for, scattered about the cellar, were no less than twenty-two corpses of men, women and children. The hardened policemen, who had all seen their share of dead bodies in the course of their work, recoiled in revulsion. Not one of them had ever seen anything approaching this spectacle for sheer horror.

Mass murder was initially suspected, but postmortems showed that there were no wounds on any of the bodies, so that was quickly ruled out. A subsequent examination of the cadavers revealed that they had all died of natural causes and then been disinterred from a nearby graveyard in Mulberry Street. Not murder then, but a thoroughly unpleasant crime nevertheless.

Within a few days, the police had apprehended most of the Hope Street Body Snatchers and brought them to justice. They each served a twelve-month prison sentence, after paying a hefty fine. However, as if often the case with organised crime of any sort, the mysterious Mr Henderson, the sick mastermind behind the plan to sell the bodies for fifteen pounds each to various Scottish medical schools, managed to evade capture.

THE PENNY LANE POLTERGEIST

In 1930, a family living in Penny Lane was startled out of its sleep by loud noises and thudding footsteps coming from the unoccupied shop next door. The source of the racket was sought, but to no avail, and every night the sound of the restless walker prevented them from getting a decent night's sleep. In the end, the tormented neighbours decided to escape the nightly cacophony and moved away, after which another unsuspecting family moved in to take their place.

The new neighbours of the Penny Lane ghost had no knowledge of the previous family's predicament and they soon settled down into their new home. Then, one night in 1945, the sounds of a heavy tread and an unearthly voice were heard. The family could tell that the sounds were coming from the shop next door but could not fathom out who, or what, could be making all the noise. And so many more noisy, nerve-shattering nights followed.

After a long hiatus, the poltergeist came out of retirement once again and, in January 1971, gave an unprecedented performance in which the family next door did not get a wink of sleep. At the time, the premises in question was a printing shop owned by Ken Shackman and John Hampton. When Ken and John had left the premises after work each night, the sounds of someone pacing the floor of the empty shop grew to such an intensity, that long-suffering neighbours complained to the police as well as to the shop's owners.

The police investigated the case with the usual scepticism they show when dealing with such matters, but drew a blank. However, Ken and John remained open-minded about the ghost and decided to research the history of the house to see if they could find any clues. They also contacted the *Liverpool Echo*.

After a journalist from the *Echo* had written a number of articles on the ghost's activities, Shackman and Hampton were inundated with letters and telephone calls from ex-Penny Lane residents who had heard the noisy spectre. These included a woman who had lived nearby when she was a child, and had encountered a supernatural entity there just after the First World War.

The woman wrote to say that one night she had heard the sound of feet clattering heavily up stone steps, while in the bedroom she shared with her four sisters. Shortly afterwards, the figure of a young woman materialised in front of her. The phantom girl just stood there for a few minutes, calmly combing her long locks of blonde hair before vanishing.

Eager to get to the bottom of the mystery once and for all, Ken and John resorted to a thorough search of the printing shop from top to bottom. They had the floorboards taken up, the walls checked, the furniture examined and the roof inspected. When the search failed to throw any light on the matter, they equipped themselves with a tape-recorder and sat up all night in the house next door, determined to get to the bottom of the mystery.

It turned out to be a night to remember.

The tape began to roll and the two brave men waited anxiously for the ghost to start walking. They did not have to wait for long … After some muffled banging and shuffling, pandemonium broke out and the walls began to vibrate alarmingly. Nevertheless they stayed there throughout the night. At the end of their frightening vigil, the amateur ghost-hunters rewound the tape and listened to their recording. The tape had actually captured the sounds of the ghost – conclusive proof that the phenomenon was not of psychological origin.

Ken and John and their neighbours noticed that the ghost was most active on Friday, Saturday and Monday nights, but why these particular nights is anybody's guess.

In time, the ghostly noises and disturbances became fainter and fainter, until eventually the nights at the printing shop became filled with an uneasy silence. Today, that shop on Penny Lane has lost its spooky reputation and subsequent residents, and their neighbours, have not reported any nocturnal problems.

But the Penny Lane Poltergeist may only be resting and may yet make a comeback.

THE GHOST OF
JAMES STREET STATION

In January 1996, Radio City presenter, Billy Butler, received a letter from James Davidson, a school lollipop man, who lived near Penny Lane. The letter was about two very strange, and almost identical encounters that he had had at James Street Station, in the summer and autumn of 1995.

Mr Davidson had been heading for Hoylake on the train at 10 o'clock in the morning on the first occasion. As soon as he had settled himself in his seat, he noticed a man dressed as a First World War officer sitting in the compartment. The man had a very upright, military bearing and his face was set into a stoney sternness, like the soldiers on the Horse Guards' Parade, who have been trained not to display any emotion, no matter how much they are provoked.

Mr Davidson was fascinated by the soldier and couldn't take his eyes off him. At first, he naturally assumed that he was either in fancy-dress – although it was a strange time of day for fancy dress – or more likely was an extra in some period drama being filmed in the area. This option was more likely, because the film industry was really taking off in the city at that time.

Yet when Mr Davidson scrutinised the man more closely, he became aware that there was something else about him that was odd, apart from the way he was dressed – a startling flatness. He seemed to be practically two-dimensional, as if he were a cardboard cut-out, yet he was just as animated as any of the other passengers, occasionally looking out of the window, or at the other people in the carriage. Yet whatever he was doing, his fixed expression did not alter.

The stern-looking soldier was one of the first people to get off the train at James Street Station. As soon as his feet touched the ground, he marched purposefully along the platform towards the out-of-bounds area at the far end, where the tunnel dips underground and leads under the River Mersey to the Wirral.

Mr Davidson and several other witnesses watched the man – carrying a baton tucked under his armpit, in the typical way of an army officer – and then stride directly towards a brick wall, walk straight through it and vanish! All those who witnessed this incredible disappearing act, looked at each other for an explanation, but none was forthcoming, other than that they all agreed that they must have just seen a ghost. "I wasn't scared," wrote Mr Davidson, "just absolutely mesmerised!"

Having seen such a spooky spectacle even once in a lifetime is unusual, so imagine how our poor Mr Davidson felt when he saw the ghostly officer repeating the eerie scene in front of another group of dumbstruck commuters in the autumn of 1995. At about this time, the *Liverpool Echo* ran a small piece about the ghost, simply reporting that commuters had seen the soldier disappearing into a wall on the underground. Research has since established that a colonel in the British Army died on the railway line at James Street Station around 1919, but it is impossible to determine from the records, whether it was an accident or suicide.

Unlike most witnesses of such an encounter, Mr Davidson made a sketch of the phantom he had seen. I have interviewed him at length and find him a very sincere and intelligent man. I have also traced two other witnesses who saw the station ghost and their accounts tally exactly with the description of events given by Mr Davidson.

FUN AND GAMES
AT THE COACH AND HORSES

In addition to the other drinkers who frequent the Coach and Horses in Low Hill, Everton, are two other spectral regulars. One of the ghosts is a dark, amorphous figure, which manifests its presence by resting its dismembered hand on the bar from time to time. The drinkers who frequent the pub are now quite used to this chilling entity and take the whole thing in their stride; they have even nicknamed him 'George'.

Christine Tierney, however, had only been the landlady of the pub for a year, when George came out of the woodwork to perpetrate a cowardly act, and she is not so forgiving. One day, she was busying herself tidying up the pub, taking advantage of the fact that her eighteen-month-old son was peacefully sleeping in his pram upstairs.

Combining motherhood with the duties of a landlady was never going to be easy, she reminded herself.

However, no mother of a young baby can ever really get any peace of mind, because even when the babies are quiet, they immediately start to worry. She went upstairs to do a quick check on him and to her horror, she found him lying fast asleep on the floor of his room, only minutes after she had put him down to sleep in his pram.

Mrs Tierney scooped up the child, who looked completely unharmed, and gave him a quick visual check over. There were no obvious injuries, but she took him to hospital, just in case, since he must have fallen out with quite a bang. The doctors could find no bumps or bruises on him either, so they gave him a clean bill of health and said that, in their judgement, he definitely could not have fallen out of his pram. Whatever had happened – and everyone who knew the place was sure that it was supernatural – the baby had slept right through the incident without coming to any harm, so that was something to be grateful for. Nevertheless, the finger of suspicion pointed firmly at George!

Shortly afterwards, Joe Downs, one of the regulars, came staggering out of the pub's toilet, a trembling wreck and his face as white as a sheet.

"Whatever's the matter, Joe?" asked the landlady. "You look like you've seen a ghost in there."

Joe was unable to speak for a good half hour and was given a double brandy to help him recover. He never did divulge what he had seen in the toilet that night, despite much prompting from his friends, and he has since refused, despite a lot of good-natured ribbing, to go to the toilet on his own.

According to people who have seen George, the

apparition looks similar to the Predator creature from the Arnold Schwarzenegger film. It is sometimes transparent, but its outline distorts the background when it moves, as if looking through a pane of flawed glass.

George's identity is unknown, but he is suspected of being the ghost of a previous landlord of the pub, who hanged himself in the cellars amongst the kegs of beer. In 1995, George solidified into the image of a realistic-looking man, who helped a female customer to stack chairs when the pub had closed one night.

Landlady Christine recalls the incident well, "When she had finished, she asked me if I was going to offer the man a drink for helping her to clear up. I had to tell her that we were actually the only ones left in the pub. There was no one else about. She was quite badly shaken, as it was her first encounter with George!"

George's ethereal alter ego was a tall figure wearing a top hat, or maybe it was one of his ghostly friends, come to join him for a night out down at the local.

HAUNTS OF THE DRINKER

The local pub has always been one of the focal points of any community, a place where people come together and conversation flows. Whilst much of this talk is often purely centred around local gossip, or the weather, opinions are also voiced on everything from religion and politics to sport. A pint of beer, or a gin and tonic, is recognised as having the effect of loosening the vocal chords, even in the shyest of individuals.

Long before the advent of the karaoke machine and the giant television screen relaying football matches from around the globe, the public house was a popular place to exchange stories, but this story-telling tradition has now all but died out. As closing time loomed, around the eleventh hour, talk would often turn to stories of the unexplained – the Devil waiting in his black coach outside the pub to take the drunken reprobates to Hell; or urban myths about hitch-hikers in the area, who were really escaped serial killers … and so-on.

Of all the tales that were told by these intoxicated storytellers, none would make you shiver more than those which involved the very pub in which you were drinking. These tales were much too close to home, although some of them were probably just tactics designed to frighten the listeners, and used by the landlord, to get rid of his stubborn clientele after closing time.

However, there are some ghost stories pertaining to pubs that are hard to explain away, because so many people who have been completely unaware that a pub is haunted, have witnessed strange things on the premises. What follows are just a few of the many examples in my archive.

The Philharmonic Pub

The Philharmonic, in Hope Street, is one of the most treasured drinking haunts in the city. Its Art Nouveau tiling, stunning glass partitions and wooden panelling are some of the best examples of craftsmanship of their kind that you will find in any public house in the country. Yet little do those visitors to the pub (often lured there out of curiosity to see the elaborate decor of the gents' toilets) realise, that the pub is also famous for something else – its ghost.

Fortunately, this resident ghost is said to be of the lucky variety, in that he brings good fortune to those who come across him. It is alleged that drinkers who have seen the ghostly shape of an old man in a grey cloth cap and shabby raincoat sitting in the parlour, have then had good luck in gambling soon afterwards – especially so with the pools, the lottery and the Grand National.

But beware, this innocuous old ghost is not the only supernatural being associated with the pub. Another, rather more disturbing visitation has also been encountered on at least two occasions very close to the pub – a banshee. This Celtic entity was first seen in February 1994, when Philip, a student, was leaving the pub with a couple of friends at around 11 o'clock at night. As he passed by the alleyway on the Hardman Street side of the pub, he heard loud sobbing. He stopped and noticed the figure of a woman with long white hair, which completely covered her face, leaning against a wall and crying pitifully in the dark alley.

Philip was a caring lad, the sort who would automatically have gone to the aid of any woman in trouble, but he somehow sensed that there was something creepy and other-worldly about this woman and so he decided not to go to her and quickly rejoined his friends. Nevertheless, his conscience kept pricking him, and he could not get the image of the sobbing woman out of his mind for the rest of the journey home.

When he arrived at his bedsit in Ullet Road, he received the second, and much more serious, shock of the night; a phone call from his mother in Kent. She was beside herself with grief, because his father had dropped dead from a heart attack – at precisely 11 o'clock that night. Even through his distress and sadness, Philip immediately made the connection between his father's death and the woman in the alleyway. He had heard about banshees before and knew that they were supposed to be harbingers of death. Could it be that the woman was a true Irish banshee? Someone who appears to those about to lose a relative or close friend?

In another similar instance, a worker in a restaurant told me that he and a friend had also seen a woman with long white hair not far from the Philharmonic pub. The two men were working a late shift on an urgent job, white-washing a cellar, when the sound of crying somewhere above them made them look up. The time was about 2 o'clock in the morning. Standing on a grid above them was an old, white-haired woman in a black dress. They could not see her face because it was concealed by her long white hair. The woman stood there for a full five minutes, before moving away at 2.05am.

On the following morning, one of those night-workers went home to find his mother lying dead in her armchair. She had suffered a massive stroke. The doctor who examined her said this had probably happened at about 2.00am, when a neighbour had heard her cry out.

The Lister

The Lister, in Prescot Road, is often visited by two of its deceased regulars, who perished in a car crash many years ago. The small matter of their deaths was not allowed to stand in the way of these two gentlemen's social lives, however, and they have been seen sitting in a corner of the pub, as large as life, quaffing phantom pints of their favourite beverages, ever since the fatal crash.

On one occasion, one of the ghosts gave a wolf whistle to a new barmaid. She pretended she hadn't noticed, but was secretly flattered – until she turned around to find that her admirer and his friend had vanished, along with their ectoplasmic pints!

The Railway Inn

The Railway Inn, in Wellington Road, Wavertree, is another pub which numbers a couple of ghosts amongst its regulars. The two solid-looking ghosts, are so life-like, that they are often mistaken for a couple of the living locals. One of them is a young man who always wears a white T-shirt, and the other is an old man in a green coat, which he never takes off.

On one occasion, a barmaid called Jennifer saw the older ghost go into the men's toilet – but it never came out again. When Dennis, the pub landlord, went into the toilet to investigate, there was no one there. The two ghosts are seen quite regularly by the staff and drinkers but no one knows their identity.

The Rose and Crown

Rather than regulars, some pubs have ghostly visitors who only put in an occasional appearance. One such talkative spook once amused locals at The Rose and Crown pub in Derby Road, Huyton, when a singer was testing his microphone before starting his act. In the time-honoured fashion, the singer kept reiterating the irritating phrase, "Testing, testing, one-two, one-two," over and over again, when a voice from nowhere suddenly added, "three!"

The spooky invisible comic has also allegedly spoiled quizzes in the pub by shouting out the answers in a raspy voice, to the annoyance of the other competitors.

The Castle

Another ghost with a sense of humour is the old woman who pays the occasional visit to the Castle, in Tatlock Street, in Everton. She looks rather like a character straight out of a Dickens novel, with her lace mop cap and black shawl. But she is a merry old soul who frequently laughs and dances whilst balancing a bottle of beer above her head.

However, she is not very sociable and when anyone speaks to her, or approaches her in any way, she immediately vanishes.

THE STORY OF SPRING-HEELED JACK

Although Spring-Heeled Jack has become part of Liverpool's folklore, his unsavoury activities neither began, nor finished, in the city. In fact, he first made his presence felt in south London, in 1837.

In Victorian times, Barnes Common, an isolated tract of land on the southern bank of the River Thames, was a place to avoid at all costs. Travellers foolhardy enough to cross the common during twilight hours, or at night, could expect to be attacked and robbed, but, despite its notoriety, there were still those who were prepared to take that risk.

One evening, in 1837, one such person, a businessman who had been working overtime at his office, decided to risk taking a short cut across the common on his way home, as he couldn't face going the long way round, because he was so exhausted. As he was passing the cemetery, which bordered the common, a figure suddenly vaulted high over the railings which separated the two, as if propelled from an invisible springboard. It landed with a mighty thud directly in front of him. Although the mysterious leaper made no attempt to harm him, the businessman turned and fled when he saw that it had pointed ears, glowing eyes and a large prominent pointed nose.

Three girls encountered the same sinister figure on the following night. Again, he made his appearance by bounding over the cemetery railings but, on this occasion, he also displayed a nasty violent streak. One of the girls had her coat ripped by him, but managed to escape, closely followed across the common by one of her screaming companions. The third girl was not so lucky and tried to scream as the unearthly-looking stranger grabbed at her breasts and began tearing off her clothes. After the attack he disappeared, leaving her unconscious.

During the following month, the leaping terror struck again. This time the venue was Cut-Throat Lane, Clapham Common. After visiting her parents in Battersea, Mary Stevens, a servant, was heading back to her employer's household on Lavender Hill. As she strolled through the entrance of Cut-Throat Lane, a tall figure, dressed in black, jumped out of the darkness and threw his arms around her, holding her in an unwanted vice-like embrace, from which she had no hope of extricating herself. Before she had a chance to scream, the stranger smothered her face in savage kisses, then roughly dipped his hand into her cleavage, before laughing hysterically. The girl was eventually able to scream, which made her assailant release her and he ran off into the darkness.

Having heard her screams, a number of men hurried to the girl's aid and, after calming her down, they listened to her account of the strange and terrifying attack. Having contacted her family and made sure that she was safe, the men immediately went back and searched the neighbourhood for the mysterious assailant, but without success.

The following night, the attacker appeared again, not a stone's throw from the house where the servant girl worked. That night, the demonic figure bounded out of the shadows into the path of an oncoming carriage. The horses bolted in fright and a terrible crash ensued, injuring the coachman who was thrown from the top of his carriage into the road. The mayhem-maker then seemed to defy the laws of gravity, as he left the scene of his crime by jumping effortlessly over a nine-foot high wall. Not long after that superhuman feat, a mysterious high-jumping man wearing a cape attacked a woman near Clapham churchyard.

Gradually, the news of the satanic superman began to spread, and the public soon gave him an appropriate name – Spring-Heeled Jack.

In February 1838, eighteen-year-old Lucy Scales, and her sister Margaret, were on their way home in the evening, after visiting their brother's house in the Limehouse area, near Green Dragon alley. Suddenly, the terrifying cloaked silhouette of Spring-Heeled Jack leapt out of the darkness and exhaled a jet of blue flames from his mouth, straight into Lucy's face. The teenager screamed, her legs collapsed from under her and she fell to the ground, blinded by the flames. Margaret was left unscathed. Jack didn't stick around to survey the results of his handiwork, but jumped high over both his victim and her sister, then landed on the roof of a house and bounded off into the back streets of the metropolis to plan his next foul deed.

A pattern was emerging – Jack seemed to especially take pleasure in molesting and terrorising young women. His next attack, which took place just two days later, was also on an eighteen-year-old girl, Jane Alsop. Jane's house was in Bearhind Lane, a quiet back street in the district of Bow, where she lived with her father and two sisters. She was spending the evening quietly reading when, just before 9 o'clock, there was a knock on the front door.

Jane got up and answered the door and outside in the shadows stood a caped man. He tricked Jane, by saying, "I'm a policeman. Bring a light! We've caught Spring-Heeled Jack in the lane!" Jane ran excitedly back into the house and obligingly returned with a lantern. Offering the lantern to the caller, she beheld a nightmarish sight. The flickering light illuminated the face of the man purporting to be an officer of the law. It was Jack himself and he grinned with malice as he studied the girl's shocked expression, as the realisation of who he was slowly dawned.

Before she had a chance to move, he spurted out a phosphorescent gas, which partially blinded Jane, then started tearing at her clothes, ripping them to shreds with his long pointed nails. Jane was a plucky girl, and punched him full square on his big nose. This gave her a few seconds' grace, in which time she managed to give him the slip, but the enraged Jack bolted after her and stopped her from re-entering the house by clutching at her hair and yanking her head backwards. His claw-like hands scraped at her face and neck, but this time, Jane's screams alerted her sisters, who came tearing out of the house and they managed to drag her away from the clutches of her attacker. The three sisters rushed back indoors, with Spring-Heeled Jack snapping at their heels and, just in the nick of time, they managed to slam the door in Jack's face.

When Jane was quizzed by the Lambeth Police Court about her assailant's appearance, she described a highly unusual individual, "He wore a large helmet and a tight-fitting costume that felt like oilskin. But the cape was just like the ones worn by policemen. His hands were as cold as ice and more like powerful claws. But the most frightening thing about him was his eyes ..." said Jane with a shudder. "They shone like balls of fire."

Two days later, Jane's description was corroborated by the testimony of a butcher from Limehouse, who had also caught sight of the villain. Coincidentally, he was the brother of Lucy and Margaret Scales – the victims of the Green Dragon alley attack.

Accounts of Spring-Heeled Jack's cowardly assaults on the terrified women of South London intensified, scaring many into staying indoors after dark, while others decided to organise vigilante patrols.

A week after the attack on Jane Alsop, Jack called at a house in Turner Street, off Commercial Road. A servant boy answered the door, and Jack, shielding half of his face with his cloak as he lurked in the shadows, asked the boy if he could possibly have a word with the master of the house. The youngster was turning, about to call for the master, when Jack made the mistake of momentarily moving out of the shadows and into the lamplight, allowing the boy to get a brief look at him.

The young servant recoiled in horror when he caught sight of the caller's bright orange eyes. During those brief seconds, he also noticed two other details; he had claws instead of hands and, under his cloak, an intricate embroidered design that resembled a coat of arms with, below this design, the letter 'W' embroidered in gold.

Like everyone else in that area, the boy had heard all the spine-chilling rumours about Jack's 'eyes of Hell'; it had been virtually the only topic of conversation in the servants' quarters all week. Summoning every ounce of power in his young lungs, he let out a terrific, ear-splitting screech and, within seconds, windows and doors all over the neighbourhood were opening, preventing Jack from making his next move, which everyone knew would not be pretty. Thus thwarted, Jack waved his fist threateningly at the boy, then rocketed over the roofs of Commercial Road.

When the boy had regained his senses, he was interrogated at length by the authorities as to the details of his hair-raising encounter. His inquisitors wondered what the significance of the embroidered 'W' could be and some conjectured that it might be the initial of the Marquis of Waterford, who was widely known as a mischievous prankster. The Marquis was also something of an athlete, but his physical capabilities could obviously not be equated with Jack's superhuman stunts. Even the fittest man on earth could not leap twenty-five feet into the air unaided, as Jack was alleged to have done many times. In 1859, the Marquis met his death after falling from a horse, but the reports of the 'Jack' continued to pour into London police stations and newspaper offices. Spring-Heeled Jack was still very much at large and the population of the city continued to be plagued by his reign of terror.

Then, for no apparent reason, Jack changed his tactics – or at least his venue – and made an unexpected appearance in Lincolnshire one evening, where he shattered the rural tranquillity by leaping over a row of thatched cottages wearing a whole sheepskin. A mob confronted the laughing leaper and blasted him with shotguns at point-blank range, but their firepower had no effect. When the buckshot hit Jack, it made a loud pinging sound, as if it was hitting a metal bucket, and ricocheted off him.

The bucolic county of Lincolnshire was obviously not altogether to his liking and he soon tired of it, turning his attentions to Shropshire. One night, in January 1879, a man sleepily driving his cart across a bridge on the Birmingham and Liverpool Junction Canal, on his way home from Woodcote, a village in that county, was startled out of his stupor when a black, hideous creature, with large luminous eyes, leapt out of a tree and landed squarely on his horse's back. The man tried his utmost to knock the beast off the horse with his whip, but the creature seemed impervious to it and managed to cling on to the frightened animal, which broke into a wild gallop. When the man finally managed to bring the horse back under control, the 'thing' darted high into the air and disappeared into the treetops.

By the end of the nineteenth century, Spring-Heeled Jack was still very much around, and the geographical pattern of the sightings of him indicated that he was continuing his westerly progress across England and was now heading towards Lancashire. In September 1904, the blackguard turned up in Liverpool, where he was first seen hurtling down from the roof of High Park Street reservoir.

Shortly afterwards, Jack gave another typically ostentatious performance, designed to signal his arrival in Liverpool, when he was seen casually clinging to the steeple of St Francis Xavier's Church, in Salisbury Street. There he bided his time, until he was satisfied that his audience was sufficiently large to appreciate the death-defying leap he was about to perform. In front of the awe-struck crowds that were jostling for position in the streets below, Jack jumped suicidally from the top of the steeple and landed somewhere behind a row of houses. The mob stampeded off to find out where he had landed and rumours began to spread that his luck had finally run out and he had killed himself.

But, of course, they had underestimated him and the assembled Evertonians were subsequently startled out of their wits, when a helmeted, egg-headed figure in white, suddenly came haring down the street towards them, scattering the crowds like Moses parting the Red Sea. As screams went up from the crowd, Jack lifted his arms, took off like a rocket, and flew off over William Henry Street.

After that memorable night, Jack made himself scarce for the next sixteen years.

Then, late one evening, in 1920, a man dressed in a radiant-white costume, was seen by scores of witnesses in Warrington's Horsemarket Street, jumping back and forth from pavement to rooftop with consummate ease. As his final piece de resistance, he cleared the town's railway station in one mighty bound and was never seen in the north of England again.

But Jack had not quite finished yet and still had one last trick up his sleeve, this time for the people of South Wales.

In 1948, the last recorded sighting of the sinister leaping figure took place in Monmouth. Locals who witnessed a strange-looking man leaping over a stream near Watery Lane, at first jumped to the conclusion that he was the spectre of a man who had drowned in the stream some time back. However, the few Welsh folk who were unfortunate enough to encounter the leaper at close quarters, swore that he was much too solid to be a phantom. He was real alright, but whether he was human or not was another question.

So who, or what, was Spring-Heeled Jack? Many weird and wonderful theories have been advanced to answer this conundrum. Some observers were certain that he was an insane acrobatic fire-eater, whilst others believed him to be a kangaroo in fancy dress! Another group thought he was a mad inventor, who had built an anti-gravity device, and was prepared to use it to terrorise his innocent victims.

To my way of thinking, the one theory that does seem to fit the facts is the alien hypothesis. If we suppose that Jack was from another planet, this would explain his alien appearance, behaviour, jumping ability and his longevity, none of which fit the human hypothesis.

The descriptions of Spring-Heeled Jack's fiery gaze seem to indicate that he had retro-reflective eyes, similar to those of a cat, which would suggest he was ideally suited to the nocturnal environment in which he chose to operate. His fire-breathing is less easily explained. Perhaps what Jack really breathed into his victims eyes was not real fire (for none of those attacked suffered conventional burns, nor did the 'fire' ever singe a single hair on any of their heads), but a type of phosphor.

Another unanswered riddle is the ultimate fate of Jack. If he was a misunderstood alien, marooned in our world, was he finally rescued by his own kind? or did he die a lonely death here? This is one mystery that we are unlikely ever to get to the bottom of, but it makes his story no less interesting for all that.

CITY FM GHOST

In the mid-1980s, City FM, the independent radio station based in Stanley Street, used to broadcast a ghost story every night on its popular *Night Owl* programme. However, one night, a real ghost turned up, and proceeded to haunt the two disc jockeys and a security guard.

It all started in the early hours of one Sunday morning. A radio presenter, waiting in the station's reception area, getting ready to go on air, suddenly became aware of the sound of running footsteps coming down the stairs from the second and third floors of the building. The presenter asked the security guard, who was sitting at his desk, who it could possibly be at that hour of the morning, when there was only a skeleton staff in the building, consisting of the two presenters and the guard.

The security guard thought it was probably the newsman going to the broadcasting booth but, on checking, discovered that the newsman had not left the newsroom on the first floor since the start of his slot. There was no other member of staff in the building, so this meant that there had to be an unaccounted-for person wandering about, probably an intruder.

The presenter and the guard decided to pursue the intruder and set off to patrol the building together.

Reaching the corridor that led to the rehearsal studios, they both noticed that the air had suddenly become ice-cold. Proceeding along the corridor, they opened the fire-door that led to another passageway. The strange icy-chill was still prevalent there too. Then, suddenly, the fire-door burst open with such force that the walls shook. They may have been two grown men, but this totally unnerved them and they stood there, exchanging anxious glances.

What exactly had they just witnessed? Neither was sure, but deciding, or rather, hoping that the newsman was playing some kind of elaborate hoax, they ran upstairs to the first floor, keeping very close together. However, when they reached the newsroom they found that their colleague was busy typing, totally ignorant of the bizarre events that were unfolding downstairs. The presenter and the guard returned to the reception area, intending to make themselves a cup of tea and then mull over the spooky goings-on, but they were in for another nasty shock: the face of a very angry man pressed up against the glass of the main entrance door.

"About time you two came back!" snapped the man, aggressively. "Wasting my time and money!"

The presenter looked at the security guard, expecting him to explain what the man was talking about but the guard was no wiser than himself.

"Sorry? I don't get you," said the presenter. "What time? What money? What the heck are you on about?"

With his face contorted with irritation, the man explained that he was a taxi-driver who had come to pick up a young woman who had phoned for a cab at about 12.30. The presenter immediately realised that this did not stack up, because there was no young woman in the building and he tried to explain this to the driver.

"I know what I heard," said the taxi-driver, but slightly

more calmly this time, realising that the two men really didn't know anything about the matter. "A girl ... calling herself Barbara ... She telephoned for a taxi about twenty minutes ago. She told me to collect her from this radio station ... City FM."

"Sorry, mate. As we said, there's no woman here. Must have been a hoax," said the security guard. "Bet you get 'em all the time."

"Bloomin' marvellous!" said the taxi driver, and stormed off back to his taxi.

"There's somebody who's heading for a heart attack any time soon!" laughed the presenter.

"Yeah! But it does make you wonder who this Barbara girl was, or perhaps it was just a hoax ...?"

The two men exchanged glances that betrayed the fact that neither of them really thought that.

At 2 o'clock the presenter went on the air and tried to dampen down the anxiety in his voice. Every few minutes or so he felt compelled to look over his shoulder to check that the ghost, to whom he now ascribed the night's events, had not made a reappearance. Everything was quiet for over an hour and he had slowly begun to regain his equilibrium when, at ten minutes past three, the studio lights suddenly went out, making him nearly jump out of his skin.

In the half light, through the studio's glass partition, he could just make out a blonde woman, dressed very prettily, who was waving and smiling at him like a long lost friend. There was nothing particularly frightening about her appearance, in fact, just the reverse, and she only looked about twenty-one. As he watched, the apparition slowly vanished and the lights came back on.

The presenter told a colleague who presented the *Down Town* programme about the phantom and all the other strange happenings that night, but his fellow DJ did not believe a word of it. Funnily enough, it was this same doubting DJ who became the second person to witness the Radio City ghost on the following night, ironically as he was presenting *The Peaceful Hour*, a programme which went out just after midnight.

At about 12.03am, the blonde spectre materialised once again and stared at him through the studio's glass partition. The DJ froze, struck dumb for almost a full hour – not the best thing to happen to a radio presenter – until another presenter arrived at the studio to take over. Only then did the terror-stricken DJ break his silence, as he told him about his encounter with the ghostly visitor.

The station's journalists quickly realised that they had a scoop on their hands and called in a group of Preston-based psychical investigators, or ghostbusters, as the media prefers to call them nowadays, to look into the hauntings. The investigators studied the case, starting by looking into the local history of the ground on which the radio station was built. They discovered that a flour mill had once stood on the same site, and that a woman called Barbara, a young millworker, had lost her life there, after falling from the fourth floor of the mill.

Numerous presenters continue to claim that the girl's ghost still walks the station's corridors and, every once in a while, she pays a visit to the studios.

A Maritime Horror Story

From receiving its first shipbuilding order, in 1828, Cammell Laird of Birkenhead has turned out many history-making military vessels, such as the American Confederate steamer, *Alabama*, *HMS Ark Royal* and *HMS Prince of Wales*, the ship that contributed to the destruction of the *Bismark*.

One of the lesser-known vessels from its once famous slipway, was the Victorian troopship, *Birkenhead*, the first iron warship to be built for the British Navy. This 1,400-ton ship carried the maximum armament and *The Times* called her, 'The fastest, most comfortable vessel in her Majesty's Service, and one that can be relied on in hull and machinery'.

On 7 January 1852, after several trooping voyages, the *Birkenhead* steamed her way to the naval base at Simonstown, a few miles east of Cape Town, South Africa, en-route for Port Elizabeth. She carried a detachment of the 74th Highlanders, which was comprised of 487 officers and men. These troops were urgently needed to reinforce the British Army units in the war with the Kaffirs and many of the soldiers had chosen to bring along their wives and children.

For the first ten days of the voyage, the soldiers had to endure gale-force winds and unusually heavy seas and many succumbed to terrible sea-sickness, but none of those aboard the *Birkenhead* could have suspected that much worse was to come. After forty-seven days, the ship reached Simonstown, where there was something of a crisis. The captain of the *Birkenhead* was ordered by the military to take on coal and horses for the troops, and then to proceed, without delay, to another port along the coast. Because of the lack of room, the horses were herded on to the *Birkenhead's* main deck.

From Simonstown, the troopship steamed for five hundred miles around the Cape of Good Hope towards Algoa Bay, near Port Elizabeth. In the early hours of 26 February, disaster struck. The officer of the watch suddenly recognised a cluster of short lights in the distance and quickly realised that the *Birkenhead* was eighty miles off course. At 2 o'clock in the morning, the troopship hit a rock, and the force of the impact sent the lookouts reeling across the deck.

A dreadful cacophony of screams filled the night air as the terror-stricken horses on the deck whinnied and stampeded in blind panic. The captain, who had been sleeping soundly in his bunk, was now on deck, still wearing his dressing-gown. He immediately gave orders for the ship's engines to be stopped and instructed his crew to cut the hysterical horses loose. As soon as they were free, the frightened animals galloped across the deck, cleared the ship's rail and plunged into the sea. The horses instinctively swam for the shore, but the surrounding waters were heavily infested with sharks and only a few escaped being devoured.

Meanwhile, the *Birkenhead* started to tilt dangerously over to starboard and then began to sink. Panic gripped the men, women and children but, incredibly, Major Alexander Seton, who was in command of the troops on the ship, managed to get his soldiers under control and soon had them standing to attention, while the civilians were running around like headless chickens, most of them having realised that there were not enough lifeboats on the overcrowded ship to convey everyone to safety.

The captain attempted to reverse his ship off the rocks, but this action only further damaged the badly ripped hull and caused the engine room to flood. Women and children were put into lifeboats and then lowered into the wintry waters. Fifteen minutes later, as the *Birkenhead* slowly sank beneath the waves, the soldiers went bravely to their end, standing to attention in drill formation. Shortly afterwards, the circling sharks closed in on them ...

The wives and the children in the lifeboats, watched in horror as the sharks tore into their loved ones and dragged them screaming beneath the waves. It is said that, even today, the sharks still congregate in the area where the carnage took place – as if they somehow know about the feast of human and horse flesh that took place there and are still patrolling the waters in the hope that such a banquet may come that way again.

How the troopship came to strike Birkenhead Rock (as it is now called) is still a mystery. Some thought that the *Birkenhead's* compass might have been faulty, possibly because of the ship's iron hull. Others blame her captain. Whatever the cause, the tragedy is remembered for the amazing courage and discipline of the soldiers who sacrificed their lives for others and we can only try to imagine how they felt as their wives and children were rowed away.

THE PRESIDENT DISAPPEARS

On 11 March 1841, the Atlantic steamship *President* sailed from New York for Liverpool. She was a prestigious ship, one of the biggest and most reliable vessels of her day. Her powerful engines, constructed by Fawcett-Preston of Liverpool, had 81-inch cylinders, with a seven and a half foot stroke, and were considered to be of cutting-edge design.

Consequently, as the steamer cut through the icy and treacherous waters of the North Atlantic, none of the passengers or crew of the *President* felt at all anxious about the crossing; after all, they were on a state-of-the-art vessel. One of the passengers was Tyrone Power (grandfather of his Hollywood namesake), also an actor, and famous on both sides of the Atlantic. Power had just completed a successful tour of the United States and was now returning to England.

In the early hours of 13 March, there was a heavy succession of knocks on the door of a house in Blackheath, London, the home of theatre manager, Benjamin Webster. Mr Webster's butler went to the door and asked who was calling at such an unearthly hour.

A voice in the dark replied, "Mr Webster! Mr Webster! I'm drowned in the rain!"

The butler thought he recognised the voice as belonging to Tyrone Power, a close friend of Mr Webster's, but was not sure if he should let the caller in, so he went up to his master's bedroom to try and rouse him – something he did not undertake to do lightly.

Mr Webster woke up and, in an irritated voice asked, "What's the matter? What time is it?"

"I'm terribly sorry, sir, but someone is knocking at the hall door. He is calling for you, sir."

"Who's knocking? Don't you even know who this fellow is, man?"

"Pardon me, sir, but it sounds like Mr Power's voice … He keeps asking for you, sir … He says he's drowned in the rain," answered the butler, beginning to doubt whether he had done the right thing in waking his master at such an ungodly hour, just to convey this garbled message.

James Webster got out of bed, grumbling all the while, then pulled on a heavy coat and ran downstairs, followed closely by his butler. The bolts of the front door were drawn back and the butler nervously rattled the key into the lock and turned it. Old Mr Webster pulled the door open and stared out into the heavy rain and blackness, expecting to see Mr Power, but there was nobody there.

This did not improve his mood, and he closed the door with a bang.

"Just as I thought – nobody there!"

Webster then started quizzing his butler over the incident. The butler ran through all the details about the mysterious visitor once again. Webster began to feel uneasy, because his butler was by no means a fanciful man, and he knew that Tyrone Power had boarded the *President* on 11 March and could not possibly be in England yet and so he returned to his bedroom feeling anxious for his safety.

By 31 March, the *President* and another ship, the *Britannia*, were overdue and an article appeared in *The Times* highlighting the fact. James Webster read the article with a sinking feeling and prayed that the *President* had not met with disaster. Another week elapsed and still there was no sign of the overdue ships. Relatives of the crew and passengers started to get increasingly worried. There was a reassuring rumour that the steamship, *Orpheus*, which had left New York after the *President*, had caught up with her and was accompanying her back to New York, because she had suffered a mechanical breakdown and they pinned all their hopes on this being true. However, on 2 April, their hopes in this direction were dashed, when the *Orpheus* steamed into Liverpool and her captain said he had not set eyes on the *President* once during his journey.

Hours after the arrival of the *Orpheus*, the *Virginia* sailed into Liverpool from New York, and her captain, when asked if he had sighted the overdue *President*, said no and then gloomily added that there was plenty of ice on the transatlantic route.

On the day after the *Orpheus* and the *Virginia* had docked at Liverpool, the missing steamer *Britannia* belatedly arrived in the Mersey, amidst great rejoicing. Her captain explained that his ship had suffered damage due to violent storms, hence the delay, but when he was quizzed about the whereabouts of the *President*, he stated that he had not seen her during the voyage, and had assumed that she had already docked at Liverpool.

On 7 April, *The Times* published a list of the *President's* passengers. There were one hundred and twenty-one people on board the missing steamship, including the son of the Duke of Richmond, Lord Fitzroy Lennox, and also the famous thespian, Tyrone Power. On the same day, *The Liverpool Albion* printed the following article:

> *Nothing whatever has been heard of the President steamer. If she had run to southwards and made for the Western Isles for the purpose of replenishing her coal, she is not yet overdue. The Liverpool steamer was, in the winter of 1839, compelled to run to the same islands to replenish her coal, and took 27 days on the passage from New York to Liverpool. Prevalent opinion is that she must have run to the Western Isles and*

that she may be expected to arrive in a few days. Indeed, there was yesterday a rumour afloat, that the Lynx had seen a steamer making for Fayal.

The article seemed to make sense, and gave hope to those with loved ones on board. It was perfectly possible that the *President* could have burnt too much fuel fighting the Atlantic storms, just as she had done once before. Then a report reached London that a special night train had just pulled into a station in Birmingham from Liverpool. A messenger on the train declared that the *President* had docked at Liverpool in a severely weather-battered state, but when the authorities in London made enquiries in both Birmingham and Liverpool, they learned that the story was a cruel hoax and the *President* was still missing. Relatives of the people on the missing steamer broke down and sobbed when they realised that some cruel joker had callously built up their hopes, only to squash them again.

When the *President* was three weeks overdue, several Irish ships coming into Liverpool brought some interesting and optimistic news with them. The crews of these ships swore that they had seen a large steamer standing off – waiting for water in the Victoria Channel – but, because of the morning haze, none of the witnesses had been able to clearly identify the mystery steamship.

The accounts given by the Irish sailors spread throughout the Liverpool docks and, that morning, the flag of the consignee was hastily hoisted at the signal station. Lloyd's of London was informed and messages were promptly sent to Tyrone Power's wife and the Duke of Richmond. The news reached the ears of Queen Victoria herself and, the following day, *The Times* reported that the Queen had expressed the highest satisfaction at the gratifying communication.

The city and the country held its breath, but sadly, the Irishmen had been mistaken, and the steamer they had sighted was the *Falmouth*, and not the *President* after all.

Around this time, a Cork newspaper reported that a sealed bottle had been picked out of the sea containing a scrap of paper. Written upon this paper was the following stark message: 'The President is sinking. God help us all. Tyrone Power.'

Having experienced so many highs and lows already, many people dismissed the newspaper report as yet another hoax, and chose not to believe the message. The last rumour about the missing ship came from a Portuguese ship. The captain said he had passed a large steamer that fitted the description of the *President* on 24 May. The unidentified steamer seemed to be disabled and was drifting in the Atlantic, with no sign of life on board.

Some of the relatives of the passengers on the missing ship never gave up hope, whilst others, being more realistic, accepted that the ship was lost forever. Many of those who had spouses among the missing, eventually remarried and rebuilt their lives. The seafaring communities on both sides of the Atlantic were completely baffled by the steamship's disappearance. If the *President* really had gone down in the storms of the 12 and 13 March, why had the vessels following the steamship, on the same route, not encountered any floating wreckage? After all, the *President* was a wooden ship.

The tragic fate of the steamship *President* remains one of those unsolved maritime mysteries.

THE ADMIRAL KARPFANGER

For over a fortnight in 1937, the magnificent four-masted sailing ship, *L'Avenir*, lay rusting and neglected in the Liverpool docks. The Finnish-owned vessel had been built in the late nineteenth century, in the era of sail, and had been used mainly for shipping grain to ports all over the world. Now, in 1937, such sailing ships were deemed obsolete and the owners, the Erikson Company, had no option but to try and sell the antiquated work-horse.

The Hamburg-Amerika line happened to be in need of a ship in which to train its officers, at that time, so when its directors heard that the Finnish ship was up for sale, they sent the head of their nautical department and a senior engineer from German Lloyd, to Liverpool, to inspect *L'Avenir*. The two men were pleasantly surprised by the large barque's condition and immediately started negotiations to purchase the ship.

Within a few weeks, *L'Avenir* was being towed from Liverpool to Hamburg, where it was to undergo an extensive refit. The ship was duly equipped with the latest engines, sonar and a modern radio transceiver. On the outside, *L'Avenir* retained the appearance of an old-fashioned barque, but the ship's interior had been gutted and was now thoroughly modern.

On 16 September 1937, *L'Avenir*, now re-christened the *Admiral Karpfanger*, left Hamburg under the power of her new diesel engines in the capable hands of her new master, Captain Walker, an experienced mariner. On board, were fifty-nine people, five officers, a navigation instructor, the ship's doctor, a crew of nine, a carpenter, a bosun, a sailmaker and forty officer cadets.

Back in their homeland, Hitler was making preparations for his assault on Germany's neighbours, but as the *Admiral Karpfanger* ploughed through the waters of the chilly Atlantic heading for the southern hemisphere, none of those on board gave any consideration to the rise of the Austrian madman. To his closest friends, Captain Walker had confided that he had a strong feeling that he belonged to the sea because, at sea, he was neither a National Socialist, nor even a German, but a mariner of the world, and he cherished this freedom.

On 5 January 1938, the *Admiral Karpfanger* dropped anchor at Port Germein, in South Australia, where the vessel took on 42,000 bags of grain. The cadets watched with admiration, as professional stevedores efficiently packed the hold of the ship with the bags, erecting wooden bulkheads every so often, to prevent the cargo from shifting during the voyage. The journey home to Hamburg commenced on 8 February and Captain Walker estimated that they would reach their home port in May, returning via the traditional windjammer route around Cape Horn.

Three days into the voyage, a German coastal radio station received a weak short-wave transmission from the ship. The signal was badly scrambled and completely unintelligible. Ten days later, Captain Walker tried to radio his position once again, but this time the transmission was unsuccessful because of atmospheric disturbance. The third message came through perfectly clearly and Walker was heard to report that the ship's position was latitude 51 degrees south, longitude 172 degrees east and that all was well on board.

On the morning of 12 March, the German radio station at Nordreich, transmitted a message to the second officer on the *Admiral Karpfanger*, informing him that his wife had just given birth and congratulating him on becoming a father. At six o'clock that same morning, the elated second officer replied by short-wave radio to the operator at Nordreich, thanking him for relaying the wonderful news. Captain Walker then radioed a message that he would make his next transmission on 16 March and signed off.

But the 16 March came and went and no message came through from the ship. The diligent radio operator listened in to the atmospheric howling and static for hours on end, but it was all in vain, and he never heard from the *Admiral Karpfanger* again. The Hamburg-Amerika line issued a statement to the German press advising that the ship's radio had probably broken down, but the faithful radio operators at Nordreich continued to listen for a message.

April went by and still no message came through and none of the vessels that had passed the barque's estimated position had had any sight of her, although the Hamburg-Amerika line was still insisting that the ship was only silent because of a radio fault.

Now it was the month of May and the *Admiral Karpfanger* was expected to enter the Bay of Biscay any day, but the days slipped by and the ship was still nowhere to be seen. Even though the *Karpfanger* had taken the consignment of grain on board in Australia, it was by no means fully loaded and was still basically a training ship. As such, the barque should have made a much faster passage than a cargo ship. Taking this into consideration, and when the whole of May had passed without any sightings of the overdue ship, the ship's owners and relatives of the crew and forty cadets became gravely concerned.

By 29 June, the missing barque's reinsurance rate was rising steadily on a daily basis. The shipping line instructed the cargo ship, *Leuna*, which was also loading in Australia, to make a return journey along the exact same route as the *Admiral Karpfanger*. Hamburg-Amerika also requested that the Argentine government use its survey ship, *Bahia Blanca*, to look out for wreckage from the missing training ship. The captain of the *Bahia Blanca* actually did spot the floating vestiges of a ship but it was not from the *Admiral Karpfanger*. The *Leuna* came into Hamburg with no news of the missing ship's whereabouts. The Hamburg-Amerika line sent out other ships to look for it, but they too all returned without any trace of a sighting.

By 23 August 1938, the training ship was declared as uninsurable on the London market and, by September, the Hamburg-Amerika shipping line had to discontinue its searches and announce, with great sadness, that the *Admiral Karpfanger* was officially lost at sea. In response to the announcement, all German ships immediately flew their flags at half-mast. It was a tragedy that cut across the boundaries of nationalism, and newspapers and radio bulletins across the globe mourned the loss of so many young lives.

The *Admiral Karpfanger*'s fate is still a complete mystery, even today. It seems highly unlikely that a captain of Walker's experience would have put his vessel on the rocks of Cape Horn, even though many a less experienced captain had done so before.

One report which may throw some light on the mystery, was largely overlooked at the time. It came from a Captain Pilcher of the British motorship, *Durham*, which had taken the same route as the missing German ship. Pilcher said he had sighted many gigantic icebergs – some up to 500 feet in height and a mile long – on the 24 and 25 of March. Pilcher added that he had never seen so much ice so far north before. In the light of this report, it seems likely that the

German training ship, not expecting icebergs at such latitudes, may have hit one of these gargantuan icebergs. Yet if that was the case, why was no wreckage ever found? The sea does not easily give up her secrets and this is yet another mystery from the locker of Davy Jones.

THE SS ELLAN VANIN MYSTERY

As we have seen in the previous story, the sea can be a cruel, and mysterious mistress, who keeps her secrets well. Her changeable nature can fool even the oldest sea-dog – like a millpond one moment, stormy the next. She has often spared the lone mariner, whilst sentencing sleek ocean liners and their passengers to an eternity within her dark, uncharted abyss.

For many years, the sea was hospitable to the *SS Ellan Vanin*, a 375-ton Isle of Man steamer that sailed regularly from Ramsey to Liverpool, Scotland and Whitehaven. From 1883, the Manx vessel was a common sight steaming through the Irish Sea and the ship's master, Captain John Teare, had the reputation of being something of a dare-devil because he was never one to be deterred by even the most ferocious weather. While other ships were taking shelter from the storm in Ramsey Bay, the *Ellan Vanin* would often be seen steaming for Whitehaven and would return in the evening to be hailed for her bravery by the whistles of the other ships in the bay.

However, one morning, the sea abruptly ended its love affair with the little steamer. On 3 December 1909, the *Ellan Vanin* left Ramsey, bound for Liverpool with fourteen passengers, a crew of twenty-one, sixty tons of cargo, eighty-eight sheep and several mailbags. The vessel also carried the usual quota of precautionary lifeboats and lifebelts.

As the steamer left Ramsey Bay, there was a moderate north-westerly breeze blowing across the Irish Sea, which promised a speedy crossing. By 6 o'clock, the breeze had picked up and quickly become a raging force-twelve gale and huge waves, higher than a house, were tossing the steamer about like a toy boat, as it approached the entrance of the Mersey. It was the worst storm in living memory. Half an hour later, anxious lookouts on the Bar Lightship, watched the distant lights of the inward-bound ship, hoping and praying that she would make it safely to the sanctuary of the Mersey.

Suddenly, there was a flash of light from the storm-stricken steamer and then all her lights went out simultaneously. The lookouts on the Lightship watched helplessly as the *Ellan Vanin* disappeared under the black icy-cold waves, taking all thirty-five souls on board with her. The fate of the steamer seemed so swift – it all happened in a matter of seconds – to the observers on the Lightship, that it almost seemed as if something had sucked the ship under.

Five hours later, the Mersey Docks and Harbour Board was informed that the Q1 buoy, anchored at the mouth of the Mersey, had been seen drifting up the river. The Dock Board's vessel, *Vigilant*, which tended the Q1 marker, was sent out to trace the rogue buoy, but the ship found more than a damaged buoy; she encountered the masts of the sunken *Ellan Vanin*, lying broadside to the tide over a thousand yards from the buoy.

Thirty-five feet of the steamer's forepart had broken off. Dozens of lifebelts, the carcasses of drowned sheep and a solitary mailbag had already been found, hours earlier, off Rock Lighthouse at New Brighton and other parts of the wreck turned up at Blundellsands. The *Ellan Vanin's* saloon clock was washed up on Crosby shore. It had stopped at 6.50am.

It was initially thought that the *Ellan Vanin* had collided with the Q1 buoy but, when investigators from a salvage vessel dived on the wreck, they found a gaping fourteen-foot hole in her port side. What had caused this hole in the vessel has never been determined.

Over the following months, several bodies were cast up on the coast, among them a young Manxman who had been on his way to Liverpool to board a ship to New York, where his late uncle had left him a fortune.

Captain William Carter of the salvage vessel, *Salvor*, was puzzled at the state in which he found the *Ellan Vanin* after the tragedy. All the passengers' doors had been locked and, although the ship's lifeboat davits had evidently been prepared for turning out, there had been no distress flares fired, which indicated that she must have gone under the waves very quickly; so quickly that there had not been time for the ship's passengers to put on lifebelts, a puzzle that has never been satisfactorily solved.

WHATEVER *DID* HAPPEN TO VICTOR?

We have all heard of mysterious disappearances, like the man who popped out for a packet of cigarettes and was never seen again, or the little schoolgirl who skipped off to the corner shop for sweets and disappeared off the face of the earth. Some are probably nothing more than urban legends, but the following tale is factual and certainly gives pause for thought.

One cold autumn night in 1920, Victor Grayson, a Socialist MP, boarded a train at Lime Street Station. Grayson relaxed into his seat and the train steamed off into the night, bound for Hull, where the MP was due to deliver one of his renowned firebrand speeches. What happened next has been the subject of much debate ever since.

When the train arrived at Hull, Grayson was not on board. The police naturally suspected foul play somewhere along the line. There were many right-wing extremists who feared that Grayson was sowing the Socialist seeds of the long-dreaded British Revolution and, without a doubt, there were many in the higher echelons of the glittering champagne society of the 1920s, who would have slept easier in their beds with Grayson out of the way.

A massive search was launched, covering the six counties between Liverpool and Hull but, after eight weeks, the embarrassed police were forced to admit that they could find no trace of the missing MP and decided to call it a day.

Albert Victor Grayson, the son of a carpenter, was born in Kirkdale, a notorious Liverpool slum area in 1881. There were many rumours connected with the future political firebrand's birth, and tales of a mysterious but distinguished gentleman, who regularly visited Grayson's mother at her crumbling house in Talieson Street.

The visitor generated a tidal wave of gossip in the neighbourhood and much was made of the fact that someone "high up" was evidently financing young Victor's education. Despite his humble origins, Victor grew up without a trace of a Liverpudlian accent and he later revealed that this was because of the elocution lessons he had received in his younger days.

At the age of twenty-five, he became Member of Parliament for Colne Valley, but lost his seat in 1910, which upset him greatly and was followed by a downward spiral into alcoholism. Upon the outbreak of the First World War, Grayson abandoned his pacifism and while he was accompanying his actress wife on a tour of New Zealand, he decided to sign up with the New Zealand Army. He fought at Passchendale and was wounded and decorated.

Shortly after the police had abandoned their search for Grayson, there was a sinister twist in the case, when Grayson's bag turned up at a London hotel. Police quizzed the hotel manager and he told them that the man who had left the bag had had his head swathed in bandages and appeared to have a badly injured arm. He had left the building accompanied by two smartly-dressed men. A painstaking search was made of the room that the mystery man had booked, but the beds and bathroom were pristine, and the room appeared never to have been occupied.

Grayson's relatives and colleagues waited for news of his whereabouts with ever-fading optimism. Some were still of the opinion that the MP had been murdered on the Hull-bound train and thrown from the carriage during the night journey, while others speculated that he had, from the account given by the London hotelier, sustained head-injuries from some type of accident and had probably lost his memory as a result. The possibility that the man in the London Hotel with the bandaged head may have been Grayson recovering from plastic surgery, was never considered, but why would the absent MP go to such lengths to disguise himself?

As the years passed by, it became clear that Victor Grayson was not going to reappear. Rumours spread that he had gone into hiding after being involved in the honours-for-sale scandal of the Lloyd George era (nothing changes!). Then a curious claim that Grayson was the half-brother of Winston Churchill was swiftly silenced in the most sinister way. No one knows who started the Churchill rumour but the smear seemed to originate in the House of Commons. It was true that Grayson bore a strong facial resemblance to Churchill but the theory still did not explain the Socialist's disappearance.

Then came news of unverified sightings, the most intriguing of which took place in London, in 1932, on the top deck of a bus! GA Murray, an old colleague of Grayson's, said he was idly looking out of the window near Oxford Street, when he caught a glimpse of Grayson gazing in a shop window. Murray almost toppled down the bus stairs in his efforts to chase after his old friend but, by the time the argumentative driver had agreed to stop the vehicle between stops, the elusive MP was nowhere to be seen.

Shortly after that sighting, another old acquaintance of Grayson's claimed he had glimpsed the evasive MP travelling on the London Underground. A grey-haired Grayson had on his arm an attractive woman, who was heard to call him Vic. When the couple left the train near the House of Commons, the friend followed at a distance, not sure if his hunch was right or not, and saw Grayson nod towards Parliament and say, with a smile, "There's the old firm". Grayson and the woman then disappeared into the milling crowds, before the MP's elderly friend could confront him.

When Grayson's mother died at her Liverpool home in 1929, curious crowds flocked to the funeral, expecting the missing MP to put in an appearance amongst the mourners, but they were to be disappointed.

The debonair, well-spoken Grayson, born into poverty, but shielded from destitution by an unidentified benefactor, was soon forgotten, as another fire-brand rose from poverty in Austria to grab the headlines. In 1939, the year Hitler plunged the world into its second world war, an unidentified individual came forward to claim Victor Grayson's 1914-18 war medals. All that is known about this person is that he, or she, was not from the Grayson family, which adds yet another facet to this unsolved mystery.

GHOSTS OF THE ROAD

The lone night driver knows only too well how roads can seem so deceptive and different during the hours of darkness. The motorist's mind at night seems more susceptible to fatigue, and our worst enemy in the night time – the imagination.

Some drivers combat their fear by turning on the car radio, or whistling a tune, others try and think of mundane matters to stop their thoughts from turning to the passing landscape of the night outside – the silhouette of a sinister-looking hitch-hiker, the shadow of a gnarled oak tree that resembles the outline of the devil … the mind is capable of imagining them all. All effects of the mind are enhanced by the way light from sodium lamps plays its subtle tricks on the psyche of the solitary motorist. But sometimes these things are not all down to imagination and there are many ghosts reputed to haunt our highways.

One evening in August 1970, a man was driving along Poulton Road from Higher Bebington, Birkenhead, when he noticed a girl with long hair, standing on the grass verge, further up the road. The motorist stopped by her, wound down the passenger window and asked if she wanted a lift. The girl did not react, so the man opened the passenger door and was astounded to see her slowly vanish in front of him. Many more unwary motorists have offered the ghost a lift before speeding away after witnessing her slow dematerialisation. Some think the roadside phantom is that of a novice from a nearby nunnery, who died in mysterious circumstances after leaving Poulton Hall. At the time of her death, the girl was emotionally in pieces over a broken romance.

On the other side of the Mersey, Liverpool's Dock Road has two phantom jaywalkers; a man in a woollen hat, who runs out in front of buses on Sefton Street and another careless individual in a brown overcoat. In February 1996, Avril, from Cheshire, wrote to me about a heart-stopping encounter she had had with the latter:

About four years ago, I was driving from Runcorn to Crosby via the Dock Road. I drove past the Liver Buildings and then on to the Dock Road and just got level with a gateway to the docks, when a man suddenly ran out in front of my car. I know what I saw and it wasn't my imagination. The man was dressed in an old brown overcoat and wore a cap. He looked very antiquated and out of place. I would like to know who this man is and if anyone else has had this experience. The gates are the first gates past the Liver Buildings going towards Crosby.

Another phantom jaywalker seems intent on causing motorists to crash by flitting out in front of them in Higher Lane, Fazakerley. In the past seven years, this dangerous ghost – thought to be a pedestrian who was knocked down in the 1950s – waits at the curb near Sparrow Hall playing fields, then leaps out into the path of on-coming vehicles.

A taxi-driver swerved to miss the spiteful spectre one October night in 1995 and almost crashed into a wall. When he glanced in his rear-view mirror, the cabby saw the shadowy outline of the ghost peeping around a wall, fifty feet away, as if it was enjoying surveying the aftermath of the near-fatal accident it had caused.

If you are travelling along the M62, beware of the phantom hitch-hiker who thumbs a lift in the small hours in the Oak Vale Park area. A long-distance lorry driver bound for Northampton from a Liverpool warehouse, made the mistake of stopping for the M62 hitch-hiker in February 1996. Snowflakes the size of goose feathers were falling at the time and Tony, the driver of the HGV, took pity on the middle-aged man standing at the roadside in Edge Lane Drive, wearing an inadequate blue cotton zip-up jacket.

The man hopped into Tony's cab and said nothing.

"Where are you headed?" Tony asked.

"Out of this city," the hitch-hiker mumbled in a low grumpy voice.

He then stared through the snow-flecked windscreen at the road ahead, still saying nothing. Tony thought the man was odd but harmless – it takes all sorts to make a world – and he drove on through the wintry outer limits of Liverpool with his anti-social free-loader.

About half an hour later, the silent passenger suddenly said, "There was a terrible crash here. Two people pressed to pulp in an Orion … Flat as a fluke, both of them … A lorry from Ellesmere Port fell on them … Squashed them flat."

Tony shuddered at the grisly account, which the passenger seemed to take pleasure in delivering. It got worse, and he recounted the gory ins and outs of another gruesome motorway accident ten minutes later.

"Two joyriders crashed at this junction up here. One died, but his body was in the way of the survivor, so the emergency services had to cut through his body to get to the other lad … It was the only way they could get to him … The survivor was conscious through the whole thing … Must be a nightmare seeing your best mate cut in half with a rotary saw."

By this time, Tony was passing Knutsford on the M6. He felt nauseated by the hitch-hiker's macabre blow-by-blow accounts of all the pile-ups that had taken place on the motorways over the years. He finally snapped and pulled his vehicle to a halt on the hard shoulder and ordered the morbid passenger out. The passenger did not flinch, so Tony bellowed, "Get out!" and, this time, the gloomy hitch-hiker got out without saying anything.

Tony drove off, mightily relieved, and turned on the radio for company. That was the last time he was going to pick anybody up – what a nutter! Shortly afterwards, somewhere near Stoke-on-Trent, he was astonished to see the same hitch-hiker standing at the side of the road. How on earth could he have travelled from Knutsford to Stoke in such a short time? he wondered. Of course, there was no way he was going to stop. Glancing in his rear-view mirror, as he passed, Tony saw the hitch-hiker jumping up and down in a rage, shaking his fist at him.

What a night! But it wasn't over yet, because, thirty miles on down the motorway, Tony saw the same man standing by the roadside yet again, which was truly beyond belief, as no traffic had passed the lorry driver in the interim.

When Tony spoke about his ordeal to his colleagues, they calmly told him that he had encountered the M62 ghost, that was all. Tony felt faint when he realised that he had invited a ghostly hitch-hiker into his cab, and made a mental promise never to do it again.

THE LOST FAMILY

The following story was briefly mentioned about ten years ago in the *Lancet* medical journal and has to rank as one of the strangest tales I have ever researched. It happened in Liverpool in the late 1970s. For various reasons, the people named and certain details, have been changed.

In 1978, Steve Jones, a man in his mid-40s, returned home to his family in Childwall after a hectic day at his office in the city. His seven-year-old son, Damon, greeted him with a bundle of drawings he had made for his father in school. Mr Jones patted him on the head and they entered the house, where Mrs Jones was watching the television.

Barbara was heavily pregnant and her eldest daughter, fifteen-year-old Emma, told her father that her mum had been having contractions. Mr Jones panicked and told Barbara to get in the car straight away, but his wife claimed that Emma was talking nonsense; she had only had a slight cramp in her leg, that was all.

The family had settled down to tea when, Mrs Jones stood up and announced, "Steve ... I think it's time!"

Steve jumped up, almost knocking the table over, and within a minute they were in their car, heading towards Oxford Street Maternity Hospital. It was a real nightmare; the contractions were getting worse by the minute even though the baby was not supposed to be due for almost a month.

At the Fiveways roundabout, the couple's car was hit by a lorry, which pulled out in front of them. The impact sent the car rolling end over, on its roof, for about sixty yards. Steve screamed when he realised that his wife seemed lifeless; blood was trickling from her forehead and it looked as if her neck was broken. The last thing he saw before he blacked out, was an upside-down face peering into the smashed-up car.

Steve regained consciousness just over a day later in Walton Hospital's neurological department, where he had undergone emergency brain surgery to remove impacted skull fragments. The surgeon shone a light into his eyes and asked him who he was.

"My name is Steve Jones," he answered groggily.

Then, through the fog, his thoughts turned to his wife and her unborn child, "Where's my wife? Where's Barbara?"

The surgeon told him everything was fine and advised him to rest. Outside in the corridor sat Bob Jones, Steve's older brother. As the surgeon came out of the ward, Bob confronted him and asked about his brother's condition.

"He was asking how is wife, Barbara, was."

Bob looked puzzled. "But he isn't married. As far as I know he isn't even going out with anyone called Barbara."

The mystery of the missing wife deepened as Steven gradually started to recover. Bob listened at the foot of his bed as his brother told him of the events leading up to the crash at the Fiveways roundabout. Bob thought that his brother was just confused because of his head injuries and told him that he was disorientated.

"Steve. You're a bachelor. You've got no family."

Steven sat up, aghast at his brother's assertion.

"What's going on, Bob? Are you trying to tell me I don't have a family? Why're you saying this? Is it a way of telling me that Barbara's dead? She didn't survive the crash, did she?"

Bob sighed and looked down at his hands.

"You're just a bit confused. Don't worry."

Steve got out of bed. "That's it, I'm signing myself out."

Bob had to wrestle with his to get his irate brother back into bed. A nurse heard the shouting and came running in with an orderly. Steve asked for a phone and one was brought and plugged in by his bed.

"You'll see who's confused," Steve snapped, as he dialled his home number. He pictured Emma reaching for the phone. She would prove he was not imagining things. "Come on, Emma, answer the phone," he muttered, as the nurses and Bob looked on with sympathetic expressions. He gripped the receiver tightly but the phone just kept on ringing at the other end – no one answered it.

"They must be at school; what time is it?"

"It's Saturday, Steve," Bob answered, shaking his head in despair.

"Look, please believe me. I have a wife, a daughter called Emma and a seven-year-old son called Damon. Please send someone to fetch them. Call Emma's school, please. Better still, I'll phone one of the neighbours," Steven said in desperation.

He put the receiver down, then lifted it and dialled again. Almost immediately, elderly neighbour, Mrs Steele, answered.

"Mrs Steele? It's me, Steve Jones!"

"How are you, Steve? I read about the crash in the newspaper. I called the hospital the other day but they said you were critical."

Steve interrupted impatiently.

"Mrs Steele, could you just confirm something? I know this is going to sound nuts but could you tell me that I have a family?"

There was a pause, then the bemused old lady said, "Of course you have a family."

"Yes! I told them, but they wouldn't believe me. Please tell me how many there are in my family."

"Well, there's you, of course, and your brother Bob and …"

"No, Mrs Steele, not my brothers and parents; my own family – Damon and Emma."

There was a long silence before Mrs Steele replied, "I'm sorry, I thought you didn't have a family, Steve."

"Yes, you know I have a wife and kids. You gave Damon some toffees the other day, remember?"

Mrs Steele was confused: "I'm sorry, Steve, but you're not making much sense. Damon? Who's Damon?"

"What are you all playing at? Is this supposed to be some kind of joke?"

Feeling threatened, Mrs Steele replied that there was someone at the door and hung up.

The surgeon came into the room and quizzed Steve about his non-existent family and assured him that his memory would soon return. Steve insisted that he was not suffering from amnesia and demanded to be allowed to return home so that he could prove his claims. The surgeon answered that it would be out of the question for at least a fortnight. However, he did allow Steve to keep the phone at his bedside. At 6 o'clock that evening, something quite bizarre happened. A young girl came into the room and gently stroked Steve's face. He awoke to her touch and saw to his great surprise that it was his daughter Emma, holding a big bouquet of flowers.

"Emma! Where's your mum?" Steve asked, reassured at the sight of his daughter.

Emma hugged him and kissed him: "What's that big bandage on your head for, Dad?"

"Never mind me, where's your mum?" Steve asked, clutching his daughter's hands tightly.

"She's in hospital. She's had the baby, hasn't she?"

"But … I thought she was … I'm so confused," Steve cried.

"You know she's in hospital," Emma said, going to the foot of the bed to study her father's progress chart.

"Was it a boy or a girl?" Steven asked, immensely relieved that the nightmare was over, hoping he had dreamt the whole episode about his brother and the nurses doubting his family's existence.

"Stop acting soft, Dad! You were at the birth. You passed out during the Caesarian and hit your head on the bed."

The door opened slightly and someone called, "Emma Jones? Here a moment, please."

As Emma walked out of the ward, Steve got out of bed and hobbled after her. He opened the door of the room and saw that the long corridor outside was empty. Deeply shocked, he felt unsteady and leaned against the wall. As a nurse came hurrying to his aid, Steve blacked out.

At 10 o'clock that night he regained consciousness. The surgeon was shining a penlight into his eye and asking him his name.

"Steve Jones. And I know I'm in the neuro-ward. She came here today. I wasn't imagining it."

"Who came, Mr Jones?"

"Emma did," replied Steve angrily, pushing the penlight from his face and sitting upright in bed.

He pointed to the bouquet of flowers lying on the bedside cabinet: "Look! Did I imagine *them*?"

"Your brother left them, didn't he?" a nurse said.

"No, he didn't!" yelled Steve. "Ask him if you want. Emma brought them in."

The nurse shrugged but then noticed the card pinned to the flowers with the message: 'Get well, Dad. Love from Mum, Emma and Damon'.

When Steve was eventually discharged, he returned home with his brother and found the house in Childwall just as he remembered it, but with no traces of his family. Emma's bedroom was empty, as was Damon's. In his own bedroom, there was no evidence whatsoever to prove that his wife had ever been there. No make-up, no wardrobe crammed with her clothes, nothing. A telephone inquiry to the vicar who had married Steve and Barbara Jones was treated as a crank call. Steve stormed into a house where Barbara's parents were supposed to live, but the old couple who lived there said that they did not know of any Barbara. Nor had the local schools heard of Damon, or Emma Jones.

Not surprisingly, Mr Jones underwent psychiatric observation and finally moved from Liverpool, because it held too many painful memories for him; memories of a happy family which had apparently been erased from reality.

If we can discount amnesia and brain injury, how can we explain Mr Jones's traumatic experience? How can we explain the bouquet left by Emma with the handwritten note? Perhaps Mr Jones was transferred after the crash from some parallel world which runs alongside our one. In this world, did Mr Jones did have the family he spoke of? For all we know, there may now be some other version of you, the reader, in this parallel world, perhaps living some entirely different life with another partner.

Cathedral Ghost

The myth still persists that ghosts are unholy and so cannot enter a place of worship, despite the hundreds of well-documented cases of hauntings that have taken place in churches of every creed.

Perhaps this erroneous myth is fostered by the bad publicity that ghosts receive from the sensational tabloids, as well as such films as *The Exorcist* and *Poltergeist*, which were very popular in the 1990s. In reality, amiable ghosts greatly outnumber malevolent ones and more and more psychical researchers are beginning to suspect that these so-called malevolent entities (such as poltergeists) are not real ghosts at all, but merely the effects of an undiscovered type of energy that emanates from the minds of overactive children.

So, if we accept that most ghosts are not the demonic monsters that Hollywood or the media paints them to be, it will not seem unusual if we hear of spectres roaming the aisles of churches and, occasionally, some of our great cathedrals, such as Liverpool's Anglican Cathedral, the largest in Britain.

The magnificent sandstone structure took seventy-four years to build and the site chosen was that of an old disused sandstone quarry, which had been abandoned in 1825. These days when a quarry has reached the end of its life, there are obligations on the owners to landscape the workings, and so lessen the environmental impact of the quarrying. However, in the nineteenth century such matters were not deemed important, and so the quarry was left as a gaping hole in the middle of the city: a mini Grand Canyon. Filling in this yawning great cavity seemed hardly feasible at the time, so the old city fathers decided to convert the excavated area into a graveyard, which they called St James's Cemetery.

One warm August evening, in 1973, Bob, a vagrant, had been sleeping in the grounds of the cathedral's cemetery, basking in the last warm rays of the sun. When he had fallen asleep the place had been full of people taking an evening stroll through the grounds, but when he awoke, a couple of hours later, it was almost dark, and the atmosphere in the silent graveyard had changed completely and it was not where he wanted to be.

Jumping to his feet, he ran up the path that led to the main gate, but discovered, to his horror, that the gate had already been locked. He shouted to several passers-by, who stopped for a moment, but then quickly hurried on after surveying his ragged clothes and scruffy appearance.

Bob decided to try the other gate, at the opposite end of the cemetery. Rather reluctantly, he made his way along a path that ran parallel to the rows of gravestones, passing many dark recesses that gave him the creeps. Reaching the gate, he found that it, too, was locked. His heart sank and he stood there helplessly for a time, with night falling fast. Then, trying to control the panic that was rising in his chest, the vagrant shook the gate and shouted for help at the top of his voice, but the street outside was now empty. Suddenly he remembered seeing a gap in the railings on the eastern terrace and hurried off to check; the idea of spending the night in the ghastly place spurring him on.

As Bob was passing a huge domed circular monument in the centre of the cemetery, he paused to regain his breath, and it was then that he heard the pattering sound echoing off the old quarry walls; a sound that was almost certainly footsteps. Just coming into view in the fading twilight, Bob noticed the shady figure of a man, walking, or rather limping, down the path towards him. He immediately suspected that he was a ghost because of his antiquated attire, consisting of a top hat and a long flowing cloak. In any case, why else would anyone, other than himself, be so stupid as to get himself locked into such a place, just as darkness was falling?

Bob didn't wait to be introduced to the ghost, and fled up the nearest slope to get away from it, then grappled his way along the top, desperately hoping that there really was a gap in the railings, and that his mind had not been playing tricks on him. A quick glance behind him had already confirmed his worst fears – the ghost was slowly and deliberately coming after him.

With the hobbling figure now less than thirty feet away, at long last he located the small gap. It was even narrower than he had remembered, but somehow or other, he was going to use it as his escape route. As the ghost was almost upon him, he just managed to squeeze through, badly scraping his chest and back on the broken iron spikes. Once out, he ran as fast as his rheumatic legs would carry him, until he was safely back in the company of the living.

When Bob had regained his composure, he was able to reassess his experience more objectively, and decided that the ghost had probably only wanted a bit of human contact, after all, since it had merely followed him and not threatened him in any way. Nevertheless, he has not volunteered to test out this theory by paying another nocturnal visit to the cemetery!

The domed temple, where Bob encountered the limping spectre, is the tomb of William Huskisson, who died from the horrific injuries he received000 when he fell under the wheels of George Stevenson's Rocket locomotive in

September 1830. One of Huskisson's legs was badly crushed in the first ever recorded train accident. Is it possible that the limping apparition that Bob encountered was actually Huskisson's ghost?

GHOSTLY MAIDENS

After correlating and classifying the data amassed from the many interviews with witnesses who claim to have experienced uncanny encounters, I was surprised at the high number of people who had reported a particular type of apparition – the ghostly maiden.

Many mainstream psychologists would undoubtedly explain away the recurring tales of ghostly maidens by seeing them as ancient archetypal desire-images, like the Lady of the Lake, who features in the Arthurian romances; or the Homeric Sirens; or even the Irish and Scottish Banshee. However, the following two accounts seem to suggest the reality of such spectral females, as having an existence totally independent of Jung's collective unconscious.

In 1970, twenty-year-old Rob, met Jimmy, a friend he had not seen for many years, at the Tudor nightclub in Parliament Street. The two men enjoyed a few drinks together and, at 1.30 in the morning, Jimmy invited Rob back to his house in South Drive, Wavertree.

Jimmy's wife cooked the two men a fine supper and at about a quarter to three, Rob said he felt tired and asked if he could sleep on the sofa. Jimmy and his wife said they were happy for him to stay the night, but there was no need to sleep on the sofa, as there was an old bed in their bedroom where he could sleep. The bed had been in the room when Jimmy and his wife had moved into the dwelling, which dated back to the 1850s.

The couple got into their bed first and soon fell asleep. then Rob got into the old bed at the other end of the long bedroom and fell into a deep, dreamless sleep.

At around 4 o'clock, something awakened Rob. He does not know whether it was a sound, or something touching him, all he remembers is that something definitely roused him from his sleep. The young man sat up and glanced over at the bed where Jimmy and his wife were quietly snoring. What he saw there made the hairs stand up on the back of his neck. A young ashen-faced woman, of around eighteen, was sitting on the couple's bed, eyeing Jim intently, without blinking. By the faint light of a street lamp that shone through the flimsy bedroom curtains, Rob could see that the silent girl's hair was raven black and long and that she was wearing an old-fashioned nightgown. But what really unnerved him, were the girl's large, dark, lifeless eyes.

Rob ducked under the blankets for a few moments, then peeked back at the bed. The sinister visitor was still there, still watching Jim with that blank expression that made his flesh creep. Again, he took refuge under the blankets. After a while, with sweat pouring from his brow, he reluctantly looked out and was horrified to see the ghostly maiden still sitting there, still concentrating all her attention on him. Rob prayed for morning to come, expecting the girl to turn her attentions to him at any second, but she never did. He dared not open his eyes again and eventually managed to fall into an uneasy sleep.

In the morning, Rob told Jimmy about the girl but his friend just laughed and said he had been dreaming.

"Honestly. I wouldn't lie to you, Jim. She was there alright and she gave me the fright of my life. Aren't you bothered?"

"Keep it down, will you? My wife's dead superstitious, and if she hears any of this, she'll say we've got to move and I can't face it at the moment."

"Okay, mate, but rather you than me. I'm telling you it was so creepy."

"Okay, I've got the message," said Jimmy, signalling the end the conversation.

The girl's identity is not known but an old woman who lives in the area says that, in the 1930s, a young woman died from meningitis in the house at South Drive where Rob stayed that night. The woman had a puritanical aunt who had kept her niece apart from the opposite sex. Furthermore, the woman had passed away on her eighteenth birthday ... and she had long black hair and large brown eyes ...

In Ferguson Road, West Derby, a young man experienced a similar phantom female in the late 1980s. The man was in bed when the figure of a long-haired woman, aged about twenty, suddenly materialised in the room. Like the South Drive spectre, the apparition seemed to be intensely interested in the man and fixed her eyes (described as jet black) upon him for a very long time. This time, the object of desire was awake during the visitation, and he experienced total paralysis as the vision started to approach him. When it was just a couple of feet away, he managed to close his eyes. Instantly, the feeling of paralysis dissipated and, when he opened his eyes, the spectre was nowhere to be seen.

Surely the woman was just a sleep apparition? Yet the man in question stresses that this was definitely not the case. This begs the question – who, or what, was the entity in his bedroom? The following possible answer may seem implausible, even laughable, but mediaeval demonologists maintained that 'succubi' – lustful female demons who seduce men – could easily assume human form and appear as attractive women! Throughout history, there have been many recorded incidents of demonic-looking entities who have tried to seduce human beings of both sexes.

In the seventeenth century, in Moray Firth, an innocent young girl confessed to her parents that she had been seduced by a beautiful Adonis who often appeared in her bedroom after dark. When the parents broke into their daughter's room one night, having heard her talking to her mysterious lover, instead of a handsome young man, they were confronted by a hideous monster, who literally disappeared in a puff of smoke. Theologians, on hearing this strange tale, conjectured that the passionate monster had been an incubus – a devil who forces sex upon women.

In this sceptical age, we do not accept such superstitious interpretations. I am merely pointing out that bedroom intruders of a demonic kind are by no means a modern phenomenon. I recently received a distressed call from Anne, of Bootle, claiming that her bedroom was haunted by an invisible entity, that had patted her bottom and even got into bed with her on numerous occasions.

Looking into the matter, I decided that the entity was something malevolent and sent a spiritualist with a good track record for removing such intruders to the woman's house and, up to now, she has not reported being harassed again by the sinister being.

THE STORY OF MAUREEN ALLEN

There are many versions of this story but the following one – which comes from the north end of Liverpool – is the original.

In May 1866, Liverpool was hit by a cholera epidemic which killed hundreds of people, one of whom was Maureen Allen, a beautiful sixteen-year-old and the youngest member of a huge Irish family that had settled in Rose Place, Everton.

Maureen was laid in her coffin and the Irish wake, with its ritual drinking, feasting and lamentation, went on all night long. Early on, on the evening of the wake, at about 7 o'clock, every member of the Allen family left the house to drown their sorrows in a pub near Great Homer Street. At 8 o'clock, Richard O'Hare, an old friend of George Allen, the dead girl's father, knocked on the front door of the empty home. O'Hare, unaware of Maureen Allen's death, was just visiting from his home in Oliver Street, in the south end of the city.

O'Hare knocked several times but, after getting no answer, was about to turn away when one of the bedroom windows opened. O'Hare looked up and saw a pretty young red-haired girl leaning out of the window, whom he instantly recognised as Maureen Allen.

"Hello, Maureen," he called. "Is your dad in?"

"No," answered Maureen. "Nobody's in. They've all gone down the road to the pub."

O'Hare delved deep into his coat pocket and took out a couple of pennies. "Here you are, Maureen, love" he said. "I've got something for you."

"Oh, I can't take it," said Maureen, backing away from the window.

"Why ever not?" asked O'Hare, puzzled. "Use it to get yourself some sweets."

"I can't open the door to anybody," she replied and closed her bedroom window.

O'Hare shook his head and headed for the pub where the Allen family was drinking. When he found George Allen, O'Hare greeted in him in his usual friendly manner and told him about his conversation he had just had with Maureen. To his surprise, George Allen stared at him angrily and grabbed him by the lapels of his jacket, telling him he thought the joke about Maureen was in appalling taste.

"How could you, at a time like this?" he said.

"Like what?" asked O'Hare, suddenly realising that everyone was wearing black and that they must be in the middle of a wake.

When O'Hare was told that it was actually Maureen who had died and that she had been dead for two days and was lying cold in her coffin, he trembled and went white. The mourners had to sit him down and give him a stiff drink.

Later, back at the Allen family's home, O'Hare saw for himself that Maureen was laid out in her coffin.

"But I swear to God I saw Maureen at the window this very evening and she spoke to me," he insisted. "As if I would start playing practical jokes at a time like this. What do you take me for?"

Upon hearing him repeat his assertion that he had seen and heard their dead sister, her four brothers attacked O'Hare and were about to throw him out of the house, when their father intervened.

"Wait a moment, boys!" shouted George Allen. "Leave him be!"

Reluctantly, the four young men obeyed their father's instructions and let O'Hare go.

"What window did Maureen look at you from?" asked George Allen.

"The bedroom window directly above the front door."

"That'll be her bedroom," muttered Mrs Allen.

George Allen took O'Hare upstairs and opened a door, revealing a small boxroom.

"Exactly. This was Maureen's bedroom," he said.

"Look at the curtains!" said Mrs Allen. "They're wide open. Yet I remember drawing the curtains in every room of the house as soon as we lost our Maureen."

"Are you quite sure you drew them?" asked one of her sons, itching for an excuse to have another go at O'Hare.

"Of course, I remember," replied Mrs Allen, solemnly. "You know it's the custom when someone dies."

"In that case, who did open the curtains in our Maureen's room, then?" asked a bewildered George, to nobody in particular.

"I told you, George," replied Richard O'Hare, gently. "It was young Maureen. I saw her."

As O'Hare finished his sentence, a cold draught passed through the house.

THE RUNCORN 'THING'

Things that go bump in the night have quite a long history. An entry in the famous diary of Samuel Pepys for Lord's Day – 5 February 1660 – closes with the following ...

After supper, home; and before going to bed, I stood writing of this day, its passages – while a drum came by, beating of a strange manner of beat, now and then a single stroke; which my wife and I wondered at, what the meaning of it should be.

Students of the paranormal believe that such inexplicable noises are the work of a poltergeist, which is a German word meaning 'noisy spirit'.

A poltergeist quite often makes its debut by rapping or thumping on the walls of the dwelling it has chosen to haunt, then usually proceeding to move objects and furniture around. The early tell-tale signs of the poltergeist's work – pens and keys, or other small objects that go missing – are often overlooked, or blamed on the mundane human trait of absent-mindedness.

However, in one case, the first thing that a woman noticed was that all the pictures hanging on her living room wall were crooked. She corrected them, then went into the kitchen to make a cup of tea. When she returned to the living room, the pictures were all skew-whiff again. Minor disturbances like this may seem funny to the untrained observer, but the work of a poltergeist can often escalate quite rapidly, until they are perpetrating some seriously malevolent tricks.

In 1979, a Berkshire pensioner living in a house plagued

by poltergeist activity, received a serious head wound that required two stitches, after being struck by a small medicine cabinet which suddenly flew through the air like a bullet, straight at him.

In fact, the eerie forces of the invisible poltergeist seem to know no physical limitation. In 1713, a German doctor who made the mistake of taking a swipe at a poltergeist with his sword, narrowly missed being killed when his entire house was demolished by the unseen entity.

One of the best documented cases of a poltergeist outbreak in the North West occurred at Runcorn in 1952. It all began on the night of Sunday 10 August, when a scratching sound was heard emanating from the drawer of a dressing-table in the bedroom of Number 1 Byron Street. Pensioner Sam Jones and his seventeen-year-old grandson, John Glynn, had only just got into bed when the scratching noise started, quietly at first, then slowly getting louder and louder. Suspecting a mouse, or a rat, they both got up to investigate but were puzzled when they did not find any sign of a rodent, or rodent activity, in the drawer. No sooner had they returned to their beds and settled down when, once again, the scratching started.

The following night, the dressing-table in Sam Jones's bedroom began to vibrate and then rock about crazily, accompanied by a succession of heavy thumps to the walls of the house. Not long afterwards, a clock suddenly shattered, as if struck by an invisible hammer and a blanket-chest, weighing half a hundredweight, rose into the air and then crashed back down. Moments later, a water-jug fell off the wash stand for no apparent reason, and was smashed to smithereens on the floor.

News of the Byron Street poltergeist quickly spread and Sam Jones's humble home was besieged by an army of the curious. Journalists, who knew a good story when they heard one, badgered poor old Sam and his grandson into revealing every little detail.

The local police refused to believe that the source of the trouble was not an earthly prankster and set traps for the mischief-maker. When these measures failed miserably, Phil France, a local spiritualist, was called in. After holding an exhausting three-hour long seance in the haunted bedroom, he came out looking pale and drained and announced, "It is definitely a poltergeist". Unfortunately, he had no idea how to get rid of it.

The Reverend Stevens, a local Methodist minister, stepped up to the breach and also agreed to investigate the case. Not long after the start of his vigil in the bedroom, he was hit on the head by a hefty dictionary thrown across the room by the unseen entity. He left the house immediately, declaring, "There is no question of this being a hoax!" But again, he was unable to offer the beleaguered pair any solution to their problem.

As the weeks went by, the poltergeist activity increased to such an extent that, by October, Sam Jones and his grandson found it impossible to sleep and had to move to a friend's house to avoid the nightly trauma.

It was around this time, that a number of sinister events occurred away from the bedroom. Three pedigree pigs on the Pool Farm, where Sam Jones worked, suddenly dropped dead. Five separate veterinary surgeons examined the dead animals, but were at a loss to identify the cause of their mysterious deaths. A fortnight later, the fifty-three other pigs on the farm also dropped dead for no known pathological reason. A couple of days after his last pig had died, the farm's owner, Mr Crowther, saw a large black cloud, about seven feet in height, moving across his yard.

The cloud was pretty shapeless except for two prongs which stuck out of its back. Three days later, Mr Crowther's wife witnessed the same cloud hovering over the farm.

The most frightening encounter with the strange cloud happened a few weeks later, when Mr Crowther bumped into the gaseous apparition as he entered his kitchen and was removing his Wellington boots. He drew back as he recognised the ominous cloud and dashed for the light switch. On his way to the switch he accidentally brushed against the cloud, and the two prong-like protrusions went for his throat! As soon as Mr Crowther switched on the kitchen light, the cloud instantly disintegrated.

One night, not long after that hair-raising meeting, Sam Jones visited Mr Crowther and asked him to come and witness for himself the strange entity in the bedroom in Byron Street. Mr Crowther was understandably reluctant after his own recent experiences, but decided to support Sam and go to the house with him. When the two men entered the bedroom, Mr Crowther was lost for words when he was confronted by the same forked cloud that had attacked him a few days ago. This time it was hovering menacingly over the bed. Moments later the cloud had evaporated.

On 13 December 1952, Mr Crowther had his final encounter with the creepy cloud. He was working in his farmyard when the amorphous vapour appeared right at his side. He noticed that it was smaller on this occasion and also lighter in colour. Two of his farm dogs charged at the cloud, barking and snapping at it. The cloud retreated and rose about eighteen feet into the air before disintegrating.

Around this time, the poltergeist activity at Byron Street suddenly came to an end in a dramatic fashion, when the fitted carpet in the haunted bedroom suddenly tore itself from the floor and unseen hands seemed to be trying to fold it up. However, the poltergeist's departure came too late for poor John Glynn. He tried his best to put the traumatic events behind him by joining the army, hoping that the disciplined life, in which you didn't have to do too much thinking for yourself, would help him forget. Unfortunately this was not to be, and he suffered a nervous breakdown soon after joining up and was subsequently discharged from the army.

Ghosts of the Sky

Not all ghosts are the spirits of the deceased. There have been reports of apparitions of numerous inanimate objects, including ships, cars, buses and even aeroplanes.

Over the years, many people in Speke have reported hearing the sputtering noise of a plane that sounds as if it is having engine trouble. One night, when the sound of this mystery flyer was heard, several residents in Hunts Cross telephoned Speke Airport to ask if there was a plane in difficulty but the air-traffic controllers were not aware of any problems, and their radar systems revealed no planes in their airspace. A local historian believes that the ghost plane is the phantom of a German plane which was shot down over Liverpool during the Second World War.

In January 1974, the skies over Liverpool were visited by another aerial apparition – a black helicopter. The first reports came from policemen on night-duty, along with several other night-workers, who reported seeing a sinister black helicopter, without any lights, racing over the city's waterfront. The authorities were quick to investigate the sightings, suspecting that the IRA might be smuggling weapons into the country. Nightly vigils were held and patrols around the docks were set up, but the unidentified chopper continued to traverse the airways undeterred. Several military helicopters were alleged to have pursued the mysterious helicopter without success. In a matter of months, the black helicopter had abandoned the skies over Liverpool for good, without ever having been identified.

Around the time of these sightings, another unidentified helicopter was buzzing about the night skies of Cheshire and Derbyshire. A police spokesman involved in the hunt for the night flyer said that the pilot's flying skills were top class. Although flying at a height of only a hundred feet, the pilot managed to perform breathtaking aeronautical manoeuvres across a hilly terrain, that was also criss-crossed with high-tension electricity lines.

On 16 January of that year, the mystery pilot landed his helicopter in a field just west of Jodrell Bank and did not take off again for a full ninety minutes. Suggestions that another chopper should be used to pursue the mystery helicopter were dismissed by police chiefs as being too hazardous and, a week later, the unknown helicopter pilot and his craft disappeared for ever.

In May 1989, a massive search-and-rescue operation was launched, after scores of people in Crossens, in Southport, reported seeing a Cessna light-aircraft come down in a nearby marsh. Police closed the Southport coastal road and emergency services searched the alleged crash site, but there was no trace of any aircraft wreckage.

At the same time, people on the other side of the Wirral Peninsula reported seeing an identical Cessna plane, nose-diving into the River Dee. Thinking smugglers were dropping a consignment of drugs, the police swooped on the area to search for suspicious packages, but found nothing. Some believe that the plane seen crashing at Southport was the ghostly re-enactment of a pilot who had deliberately crashed his plane on to the beach in an act of suicide, after he had been jilted by his girlfriend.

Another phantom plane has been seen flying along the Towys Valley between Llandeilo and Llandovery in Dyfed, Wales and has been identified as a Wellington Bomber. In 1979, Martin Green, a writer who lives in the area, was walking along the A40 valley road, when he noticed a huge dark plane flying towards him at tree-top level. The strange thing about the plane was that it was silent, even though it was so close and its propellers were spinning furiously. As the plane got nearer, Green could see that it was a Wellington and watched it fly overhead and into the distance. When he reached the local pub, he mentioned the sighting of the plane and several people said that they too had seen it – but none of them suspected that it was an apparition, until Green decided to investigate.

He discovered that only one Wellington Bomber was still in existence in Britain, and that was on permanent display in the RAF Museum in Hendon. Several weeks after Green's sighting, four other people saw the same silent plane flying eerily across the valley and many others have seen the apparition since then. Wellington Bombers did train over the Brecon Beacons and the Black Mountains, near to the Towys Valley, during the last war, and it appears as if they are still flying there even today.

On Christmas Eve 1946, two Americans stationed at Burtonwood Airbase were returning to their billet after a night out at a local pub, when they encountered a human-shaped 'cloud' walking towards them. As it got closer, the two Americans could make out that the figure was a headless airman. The spectral airman walked past the terrified men and into a hangar. The same headless ghost was seen again shortly afterwards by another military man and also by a group of women who were returning from a dance at a nearby club. The women fled from the apparition, screaming.

The identity of the airman is thought to be that of a pilot decapitated when his plane crashed into a hanger at the airbase in 1944.

GHOST FAMILY OF GROVE STREET

One night in January 1980, a young woman, Susan, was walking down Grinfield Street in Edge Hill, towards the Oxford public house, when she noticed the silhouetted figure of a woman wandering about in the field behind the pub. The woman was carrying a basket, had her hair tied up in a bun and wore a long, old-fashioned dress, pleated at the waist. As Susan stared at the silhouette, the woman glanced directly back at her, before turning round and running towards St Stephen's Church at the top of Grove Street.

Susan entered the pub and was about to tell a friend about the strange woman, when she overheard a man in the parlour talking about a woman he had seen in the field at the back of the pub in funny, greyish clothes. The man said that the woman kept stooping down, picking something up out of the grass and putting it in her basket. Then, after glancing at his watch for a second, he looked up and found that she had vanished.

The other drinkers in the pub just laughed and insisted that he was imagining things, although Susan was able to confirm his story in every detail. The next day, out of curiosity, he inspected the part of the field where he had seen the grey figure and discovered clusters of toadstools sprouting amongst the grass.

Grove Street's grey lady is not alone in her field. She shares it with thirteen other apparitions! One, a diminutive flute-player who sits under an old oak tree in front of St Stephen's Church, has been seen and heard by many people over the years and some swear that his appearance usually portends a streak of misfortune.

In the public house situated at the end of the haunted field, a man known for his honesty was in the pub's empty parlour one night, when he suddenly noticed an odd pair sitting at a table over in the corner. The man was old and stooped and wore a trilby and raincoat and he was obviously with, although they didn't communicate, a girl of about twelve. The pair sat there for a few moments with totally expressionless faces – then vanished.

Towards the end of Grove Street, in Cambridge Street, late-night revellers have reportedly heard the sound of unseen hooves. The invisible steed is said to gallop from the grounds of the university, to Lully Street, where the galloping comes to an abrupt halt.

In February 1975, a field adjacent to Lully Street became the setting for a sinister spectacle that was witnessed by residents in a nearby block of flats. At about 12.45am, a couple getting ready for bed, noticed the glow of a fire in the centre of the field facing their flat. At first, they thought that someone was burning rubbish, but then they noticed nine extremely bulky black cats sitting in a perfect circle around the fire. Within a few minutes, bedroom windows were opening all over the block of flats and bemused faces looked down at the strange circle. Then, at 1 o'clock, the fire in the field rapidly dimmed to a faint ember and the black cats could no longer be seen.

Why Grove Street should have such an abundance of spectres is unknown but recently, another unexplained incident, which was reported in the *Liverpool Echo*, occurred in the same area.

In 1988, two policemen were walking their beat when they came across an old, expensively-made coffin, in a car park at the top of Grove Street. The police were relieved to find that the velvet-lined coffin was unoccupied but were obviously perplexed at finding it in the middle of the car park. The coffin was later deposited in the lost property room of Admiral Street Police Station, where, admittedly, they do get some bizarre items handed in, but this was definitely their first coffin.

Perhaps the coffin had been stolen from an undertakers, as some sort of a sick practical joke. But no one of that profession ever came to claim it and nor, by the way, did any dawn-fearing vampire, or weary zombie.

Devon Street's Reformed Gambler

For many years I have tried to track down the originator of the following tale. Many people, particularly in the north end of Liverpool, have heard about the ragman who had a supernatural experience in Elizabeth Street, Edge Hill, early last century, but the origin of the story is a mystery.

Most people I have talked to claim that the incident occurred in the autumn of 1901. This consensus was most interesting, because my grandmother had also mentioned that year when she had related to me the tale of a rag and bone man called John Irving.

Late one afternoon, in November 1901, John Irving pushed his old hand-cart out of the backyard of his home in Devon Street and threaded his way through the alleyways that led out on to the cobbled roads crying, "Any old rags? Rag and bones. Any old rags?"

Irving was an inveterate gambler who had a habit of squandering his meagre earnings on cards, drink and horse-racing, instead of supporting his wife and family. On the rare occasions when his gambling paid off, he would go missing for days on end, often returning home in a drunken and violent state, without a penny in his pockets. His wife, a timid, uncomplaining woman, never deserted him, however.

At about 4.30 on the afternoon in question, a dense fog rolled in from the Mersey and Irving dropped the handles of his hand-cart and pulled up his coat collar to keep the chill out. As he did so, he thought he heard footsteps behind him. He turned round and peered into the swirling fog, waiting for someone to show himself. The footsteps got louder, then stopped and the dark outline of a stationary dog became visible. Irving shuddered. The dog, which was black and of an indeterminable breed, seemed to have a human-like face.

"Go on, shoo!" Irving shouted at the sinister-looking hound, but the dog stayed planted where it was and its peculiar face seemed to break into a grin. The ragman grabbed the handles of his hand-cart and moved off at a pace through the lonely, foggy street, afraid to look back, lest the creepy canine should be following. Moments later, the sound of approaching footsteps resumed.

Irving was halfway up the street, contemplating whether he should try and make a run for it, when the roar of a fog-horn blasted through the air. The ragman's heart pounded when, as the echo of the fog-horn died away, the thudding footsteps could still be heard tracking his own. Irving suddenly lost his bottle, let go of his hand-cart, and ran to the nearest house, where he hammered on the front door. He then waited anxiously, expecting the eerie dog to catch up with him but it was nowhere to be seen. The front door of the house creaked open slightly and an old maid peered out at the ragman.

"Er, would the master of the house have any old garments, or the like, that he wants to be rid of?" Irving asked, removing his cap.

"At this hour? Come back tomorrow," snapped the old maid, haughtily.

"Please," Irving begged, clutching his cap over his heart. "My wife is ill and I have no money to buy her medicine."

After a long silent pause, during which the maid looked him up and down, she said, "Wait there a moment," and closed the door on him. Irving waited nervously. The fog was getting thicker and the street was as quiet as the grave. Then the front door of the house suddenly opened again, startling him.

"Come in," said the maid.

"Thank you," replied Irving, stepping into the house.

The maid led him down a long, dimly-lit hallway and into the parlour, where an old grey-haired woman with a hawk-like nose was sitting at a sewing table, engrossed in her embroidery. She looked up at Irving and smiled.

"Good evening, ma'am," he said, bowing obsequiously.

"Good evening. Looks like a pea-souper out there!" she remarked in a friendly enough way.

"It is, yes, ma'am. Fog's thick enough to cut with a knife," replied Irving, eyeing up the luxuriously furnished room.

"Fetch the cast-offs, Margaret," the woman ordered, then turned to Irving and said, "Pull a chair over to the fire, you look frozen."

"Thank you, ma'am, you're very considerate."

Irving positioned a heavy mahogany chair, that was standing in a corner, in front of the blazing coal fire and sat down on it, feeling rather like a fish out of water.

"There, finished!" exclaimed the woman, with evident satisfaction, surveying her completed piece of intricate needlework.

"Very nice, ma'am," praised the ragman, leaning over to inspect the embroidered image of a rose. "Never seen anything as life-like. You must be an artist."

The old woman laughed, lifted the lid of the sewing table and placed her folded embroidery, needles, pin-cushion and thimble inside its various compartments. She then surprised Irving by taking out a pack of playing cards from another compartment in the sewing table.

"My late husband's," she said, by way of explanation, staring at the pack. "How we whiled away the long hours of the winter evenings with a game of whist."

"I indulge in a game myself, from time to time, ma'am," admitted Irving, "Although I don't like to make a habit of it, of course."

"Really? That is a coincidence. If you wish, we could enjoy a game of whist until the maid returns," suggested the woman, removing the cards from their box.

"Er, whist is a bit too highfalutin' for me, ma'am. Poker's my game," said Irving, awkwardly.

"Then poker it is!" declared the woman, shuffling the cards and then dealing them quickly and skillfully.

After the first game, she pointed over to a small mahogany cabinet by the wall.

"Have a drink," she offered.

"Don't mind if I do, ma'am," said Irving, scarcely able to believe his good luck.

He walked over to the cabinet and pulled open its doors. His eyes widened at the sight of so many bottles of top quality whisky, gin, port and rum. The ragman grabbed a tumbler and poured himself a generous measure of the latter.

"Bring the bottle over to the table, if you wish," said the woman. "I'm a teetotaller myself. My husband was the tippler of the house."

The hours flew by, until the clock on the mantelpiece started striking midnight.

"Is that really the time?" exclaimed the ragman, "I'd better be going!"

"Just one more game," pleaded the woman. "You've won every game tonight. You must let me win the last one."

Although he was thoroughly intoxicated, the ragman felt uneasy. There was something wrong here, but he couldn't quite put his finger on it.

"The maid's taking her time, isn't she?" he asked suspiciously.

"Oh, she'll be down in a moment. Sit down and deal, please. I won't feel right letting you out into the foggy night in that state."

Irving gathered up the cards.

"Alright. One more game, but then I'm off."

As the ragman was shuffling the pack – rather clumsily because he was intoxicated – one of the cards fell on the floor. He bent down to search for it. It was not under the table, so then he looked under the woman's chair.

"No! Leave it!" snapped the woman, suddenly agitated.

Irving suddenly noticed the corner of the card, protruding from the bottom of the woman's ankle-length dress. He dared to lift the dress from the floor a couple of inches, in order to grab the card. On doing this, he instantly noticed that she did not have human feet, but cloven hooves – like the Devil. The shock of this revelation made him pass out.

When he came to, he found himself in a dark, derelict house. Getting unsteadily to his feet, he ran over the bare floorboards and out into the hall and tried to open the front door. The wood of the door-frame was in such a rotten state that the door fell on top of him but he suffered nothing worse than a bruised arm. His cart was still outside the house where he had left it, but he decided to abandon it and ran home to Devon Street in a very sorry state.

The experiences of that night turned John Irving into a reformed man overnight. He shuddered at the sight of a poker game, became a teetotal family man, and attended church every Sunday thereafter.

PEEPING TOM

The following story was investigated by a paranormal research group based in Hunts Cross and it concerns a creepy peeping tom who decided to abuse his unusual psychic talent in the pursuit of his perversions. And beware, because this sinister voyeur is still active!

For centuries, mystics and occultists have claimed that each of us has a spirit-like entity, known as the astral body, stowed away inside our physical body. This astral body is said to contain the soul, the consciousness and the 'third eye'. It is thought that some people can project their astral bodies out of their physical body and so be able to view things which are happening miles away.

Out-of-body experiences are also thought to take place when a person is in very bad health, or close to death. However, according to many yogis and mystics, we can all project ourselves out of our bodies with regular practice at meditation, but it is considered to be a very dangerous exercise, because there are reports of some people being unable to get back into their bodies after projecting themselves out of them.

If you think that all these claims about an astral body are bunkum, think again, because the CIA, FBI and several police forces in the United States and Europe have admitted that they are employing so-called, 'remote viewers' – experts who know how to project their consciousness out of their bodies, so that they can view events taking place anywhere in the world. The CIA has admitted using remote viewers to spy on nuclear missile installations in the heart of the old Soviet Union and even NASA has admitted that they have employed remote viewers to see if they can find out data on other planets. Remote viewers have even been used successfully by the police in the location of the bodies of murder victims and missing people.

There is also said to be a remote viewer living in the Liverpool area, who is allegedly abusing his psychic ability, in order to spy on women in their homes and workplaces. For legal reasons, he cannot be named, but paranormal investigators claim to know his identity. We'll call him Russell.

In August 1997, Josephine, who works for a chemists in the city centre, was enjoying a lunchtime meal at Wetherspoons, a large pub in Charlotte Row, when a small, middle-aged man, wearing yellow-tinted spectacles, came over and addressed her, as if she were a long lost friend,

"Hi, Jo!" he said. "Long time no see!"

Jo stopped eating and asked, "Who are you?"

"Russell," he replied, with a sinister sneer and sat opposite her at the table.

"I'm sorry, but I don't know you," said Jo uneasily.

"Oh! I know you don't know me … but I know you," retorted Russell.

"What do you mean?" replied Jo, feeling decidedly intimidated by the stranger.

"I saw you cutting your toenails on your bed last night, just after you got out of the bath. But you shouldn't use your fellah's razor to shave your legs, y'know. He has to use that razor himself."

"Are you some sort of pervert? I'm going call the police, right now," Jo declared furiously.

"Calm down, Jo. You're reading too much Stephen King. You're up to page fifty-six of his latest book, aren't you? I visit you every night and you can't see me. I've even seen your cheeky little birthmark," he tittered.

Russell described the exact location of the birthmark on a very private part of Jo's anatomy. She snapped and threw a butter knife at him. Then, as one of the staff came over to see what was going on, Russell ran out of the pub, laughing. Jo did not know what to think. She wondered if this Russell bloke was watching her with binoculars, or a telescope, possibly from the block of flats facing her home. Now she came to think of it, two years ago, her friend had spotted a man in those flats looking at her with an enormous reflector telescope, but Jo knew that a peeping tom, even with a telescope, could not see right into her bathroom, it had frosted glass in the window for a start. And he definitely couldn't see behind the drawn curtains of her bedroom, unless he had supernatural powers ...

The whole creepy meeting had left a very nasty taste in her mouth and she talked to her friends about it as soon as she got back to work. They advised her to contact a group of paranormal investigators who had recently been featured on local radio, because they too thought it could not be explained in any other way.

The investigators told Jo that they knew of an eighteen-year-old girl in Liverpool who was also getting strange telephone calls and letters from a guy who claimed he could visit her in his astral body. The pest had also said his name was Russell. Unfortunately, the research group said that they could not do anything about the psychic peeping tom and advised her to move to another area.

Jo convinced her boyfriend that she wanted to move to a flat near Sefton Park and he reluctantly agreed. However, the move made no difference; Jo was still under supernatural surveillance and a week later, she was in a shop in Bold Street when she felt a tap her on the shoulder.

It was the dreaded Russell.

Jo was dumbfounded as the stalker casually remarked, "Your other flat was much better. The place you're in now is facing away from the park. Isn't that Mrs Davies a nosey old neighbour? She puts a glass against the wall and listens to you and your fellah – especially when you two ... you know ... make love ..."

"That's it, I'm going to the police," snapped Jo. "There are cameras in this store taping you right now, so they'll know exactly what you look like."

Russell giggled, oblivious to her threats.

"Hey, your fellah isn't very adventurous between the sheets though, is he?"

At this Jo lost her cool and picked up a pan and whacked Russell on the head with it.

"You nutter!" he yelled, as ran out of the store.

At work the next day, Jo's friend, Lisa, waltzed up to her and confronted her. "You're a real two-faced, gossiping, little backstabber."

"What're you talking about?" asked Jo, completely baffled.

"You know quite well what I'm talking about," Lisa replied, "I got a phone call from this fellah last night and he said you and your fellah were slagging me off and saying I slept with three different men behind my boyfriend's back. You little backstabber!"

"Who told you all this, Lisa?" asked Jo, her face going bright red.

"Russell, this fellah who says he knows you," Lisa replied, taking a swipe at Jo with her handbag.

A highly undignified fight ensued, in which both girls ended up dragging each other around the shop by the hair, until a supervisor and a customer intervened.

When Jo returned home, she burst out crying. She *had*

said all those things about her friend Lisa and talked about her to her boyfriend but had forgotten about the accursed eavesdropper, Russell. Unfortunately, this story has no pleasant ending, because Russell is, by all accounts, still roaming about the city, spying on women. So cover yourself up tonight, ladies and be careful what you say about your friends ... because someone just might be listening ...

A Picture of Evil

Early in March 1995, a young couple, Denise and Joe, moved into a house in Liverpool. The house dated back to early Victorian times and had a homely welcoming atmosphere and enjoyed panoramic views of the river from one of the upstairs windows.

A fortnight after they had moved in, the couple heard strange noises coming from the attic. Denise was naturally scared but Joe pointed out that it was probably just the wind rattling the old window panes, or getting under the slates and he went up with a torch, just to make sure. He was right, the wind was rattling the loose frame of the skylight and a couple of loose slates; there was nothing ghostly about the sounds after all. Reassured when he called down to her that all was well, Denise climbed up into the attic too.

"God, this place has a real musky smell," remarked Joe.

"Yeah, probably no one's been up here for years."

Noticing a large wooden tea-chest, Denise grabbed the torch and, aiming the beam at the chest, wrenched open the heavy lid. The box contained bundles of cobwebbed documents and two pictures framed with ornate gold borders. One was of a slim man of about thirty, with dark hair and a Van Dyck beard, the other was of a plump-looking woman with honey-blonde hair and a cheerful, rosy-cheeked face. As Denise shone the torch at these paintings, the attic door suddenly burst open and a terrific howling sound, like a gale-force wind, whistled through the doorway. The door then slammed shut again with such a force that dust and loose plaster rained down from the ceiling.

"Let's get out of here, Joe. I don't like it a bit."

"It's okay, Denise; it was just a draught, like I told you."

Denise swore. "That was no draught! Let's get out of here, right now!"

She dropped the paintings back into the tea-chest and scurried back down the attic stairs.

In bed that night, Joe was soon fast asleep but Denise lay awake, startled by a distinctive creaking noise, the sound of a loose floorboard – right outside their bedroom door. She peered over the duvet, staring in horror as the handle of the bedroom door twisted and it slowly creaked open a few inches. She screamed and shook Joe awake.

"Someone's outside on the landing. They've just opened the door," she gasped.

"Don't go!" Denise pleaded as Joe went over to the door and took a peep outside. He looked both ways but there was only darkness in either direction. However, he did notice that peculiar musky smell again. Assuming that the gales outside had opened the door, he grumpily returned to bed.

A few days later, when Joe was at work, Denise was lying in bed suffering from influenza. Feeling really ill and aching all over, she tried to read a book but couldn't concentrate. She lay there listlessly, feeling very sorry for herself, until, at around three in the afternoon, something weird began to happen. Denise heard the faint sounds of music coming from somewhere nearby. She propped herself up and listened to the faint strains of a harpsichord.

Suddenly, a strange darkness came over the room. All light from the bedroom window seemed to fade, as if a black cloud had descended over the house, so dark she had to switch on the bedside lamp. To her horror she heard the floorboard creaking outside her bedroom door. At that precise moment, the bedside lamp went out with a clinking sound, as if the bulb had blown.

Denise felt cold fear coursing through her body. She sat fully upright in bed, staring at the bedroom door, as the handle began to turn, just as it had done the other night. She felt her heart pounding as the door inched open, wider and wider and wider …

As the figure entered the room, Denise recognised him immediately as the man depicted in the oil painting in the attic. He had straight black shoulder-length hair, dark menacing eyes under thick eyebrows, a Van Dyck beard and a black velvet coat with white cuffs. She was so afraid, she was rendered speechless.

The stranger opened his mouth to speak, revealing a set of yellow crooked teeth. In a refined voice he whispered, "Hello, miss." He walked across the room and leaned over Denise. Terrified, she found she could not turn away. The man's dark eyes seemed to have a hypnotic pull on her. She noticed the dank, musky smell he gave off, the same odour of decay that had greeted her when she had opened the large tea-chest in the attic.

The stranger stooped down and kissed Denise's face. She trembled as his ice-cold dusty face pressed against hers, his beard and moustache bristling against her cheeks as he tried to caress her. Suddenly, the intruder announced, "Oh, to be alive again! That would be something …" and he savagely kissed her again and then bit into her neck. Denise suddenly regained the power to move and, picking up the bedside lamp, tried to hit her attacker on the head with it.

The stranger looked up, his eyes glaring at hers with a look of undiluted evil. He clenched his crooked teeth and snarled, "Don't you dare, missy!"

At that moment, the doorbell rang out and the startled stranger fled from the bedroom in one fleeting movement, like a shadow. Denise ran out of the bedroom in her nightdress and almost fell down the stairs. She opened the door and saw, to her relief, that it was Joe, who had been sent home because he, too, seemed to be coming down with the flu and had forgotten his keys.

When Joe saw the state she was in – and the large lovebite on her neck, he became concerned.

"Denise? What's going on?" he demanded.

Denise gave him a blow-by-blow account of the assault and said she was leaving the house that very moment, flu or no flu, but Joe persuaded her to stay until he had telephoned the police. Having searched the house thoroughly to find there was no stranger on the premises, the police gently suggested that since Denise had a high temperature, and had probably hallucinated the whole incident.

"Then who did this to me then?"she screamed, pointing to the livid red lovebite on her neck.

The police said nothing but one of the officers glanced at Joe and smiled slyly.

"Don't look at me. I didn't do it," said Joe indignantly and showed them to the door.

That evening, Joe and two of his friends searched through the entire house with a fine-toothed comb. One of his mates, Alex, opened the tea-chest and had a good look at the paintings.

"What are these?" he asked.

Joe recalled that Denise had told him that the attacker had looked exactly like the man in the painting.

"One's of some weird-looking fellow and the other's of a woman."

"No, this one's blank," Alex replied and showed the painting to Joe.

There was nothing left on the canvas except a dark green background. The man with the Van Dyck beard had vanished from the painting. Joe tried to rationalise this inexplicable twist to the affair and wondered if a fungus had corrupted the painting since it had been exposed to the air, but his brain told him that that was impossible. On the back of the painting, a label with faded writing said, 'Richard Brownrigg, musician'.

Joe remembered that Denise had heard the eerie harpsichord music just before the man had come into her bedroom and, that night, the couple left to live with her parents until they could find accommodation in another area of the city. The house where they lived is still said to be haunted, according to the present residents, although they are not aware of any weird paintings in the attic.

Not long after the couple had left, at 2 o'clock in the morning, the faces of a dark, bearded man and a blonde woman were seen staring out of a second storey window ...

Bernie with the Broken Neck

This incident allegedly took place shortly before Christmas, one snowy night in the 1970s. It was one o'clock in the morning and Brownlow Hill was deserted. A light snow was falling and settling on the ground but one person who was out at that hour seemed unaffected by the chilly weather. Mr Smith, a Liverpool businessman, trudged wearily up the icy flights of steps in Brownlow Hill that led to the Metropolitan Cathedral's main square. As he reached the top, his footsteps echoed in the silence.

The businessman stopped in his tracks and took out the keyring given to him by his wife just three years ago. He had stopped at the very place where he and Melanie had walked on the night of their first date. He had met her at the Augustus John pub, when they had both been students at Liverpool University. He had always been sceptical about true love until he met Melanie. She soon moved into his flat and they married less than a year later. Tragedy closely followed, when Melanie died from a brain tumour and it cut through him to think of his wife's suffering. Unable to come to terms with her loss, he found himself on this freezing December morning at the very spot where he had once found such happiness.

Mr Smith climbed up on to the snow-covered wall that bordered the square and prepared himself to jump down into the crypt, some 50 feet below. Life was unbearable without Melanie, and he could not face another desolate Christmas without her. He closed his eyes and was about to jump, when someone shouted out behind him. He looked around in surprise, having thought he was alone.

"Don't!" shouted a scruffy-looking man, standing in the

square behind him, and stretched out his arms to the would-be suicide.

"Shut up! Beat it!" said Mr Smith, breaking down.

The tramp stood his ground.

"No, I won't. It isn't right. Just because your little world is falling apart. That's the coward's way out!"

Mr Smith shouted a string of four-letter words and ended with, "I don't want to live, so just please leave me alone."

"Okay, friend, but have you ever wondered what will become of you if you do decide to jump?"

"Yes," said Mr Smith, "I'll be dead, that's what'll become of me."

"A child knows that," persisted the tramp, "but what if that isn't the end?"

"You're drunk, just leave me alone," snapped Smith and he turned back to contemplate the glistening ground below.

"You mightn't even die if you fall down there," the tramp chuckled.

"Look, just go, will you?"

But the tramp stayed put and rambled on, "You could smash your head in and end up like a cabbage. You'd have to be spoon-fed for the rest of your life ..."

Mr Smith took a deep breath and started to sway back and forth slightly.

"... Even if you smash your brains in and your organs fly everywhere, you might still take a few minutes to die," added the tramp, "and you know when you're lying there after the fall and you're barely alive, all your organs are ruptured and your blood is spreading into a great big puddle, you taste your own salty blood in your mouth and you are seized by this terrible panic and you change your mind and suddenly want to live. You hope and wish that it's all just a bad dream but it isn't ... you realise that you're going to die."

"And how come you know all this?" Mr Smith asked, momentarily diverted from his own misery.

"I'll give you a clue," grinned the tramp and tilted his head until his ear touched his shoulder.

Mr Smith shuddered when he saw this gruesome contortion act. Surely the fellow was just double-jointed. The tramp then flipped his head right back in one swift movement, so that the back of his head touched his shoulder blades. With a sense of mounting horror, Mr Smith realised that no one – not even someone double-jointed – could flip his head back like that. The tramp turned around on the spot and his dangling head swung about as if his neck was broken.

With his face upside down, he smiled, "I jumped ... Look what happened to me ..."

Mr Smith got down off the wall, trembling, and ran across the square in a state of fright. He turned back once and saw that the tramp had vanished. The businessman hesitated and looked in the snow. There was his own trail of footprints but there was no trace of any footprints leading to the spot where the vagrant had appeared. He hurried down the stairs then raced up Brownlow Hill. It had stopped snowing and a full moon had emerged from a break in the clouds. He glanced back towards the cathedral and saw a solitary shadowy figure coming down the steps in the moonlight. He could not be sure, but the figure looked like the tramp with the broken neck. Horrified, he realised it was heading his way. He had to get away from him, so he hailed a black cab which took him safely back to his home in Old Swan.

The chilling experience left Mr Smith with no further desire to end his life and he gradually pulled himself out of his depression.

In the February of the following year, he read an interesting article in the *Liverpool Echo*, which reported that a group of tourists visiting the Metropolitan Cathedral had encountered the ghost of a shabby-looking man in its main square. After smiling at the Americans, the man had vanished before their startled eyes. A ghosthunter looked into the case and found that many other people had seen the same solid-looking bedraggled phantom. A medium who was brought in to make contact with the ghost, claimed that the apparition was Bernie Brown, who had died in the Liverpool Workhouse in the nineteenth century, after breaking his neck jumping from a window. This seemed to fit the facts, because the cathedral was built on the site of the old Liverpool Workhouse.

So if you're travelling near Brownlow Hill tonight … watch out for Bernie with the broken neck.

THE HARRINGTON SCHOOL VISIONS

The German writer, Goethe, once asserted that an evil or tragic event sometimes gives a warning of its approach by casting its shadow ahead of its path. Goethe was talking about premonitions – supernatural warnings of a dire future event, which may take the form of a hunch, a nightmare, or even a vision – as I will recount later in this chapter. Scientists say that, by all rational criteria, premonitions are impossible, because the future has yet to take place, but there have been well-documented instances of premonitions that are hard to explain with our present scientific knowledge. One example occurred on 20 April 1889, when a young Austrian, Klara, went into labour.

The old midwife who attended Klara had delivered countless babies but when she delivered Klara's baby, she felt clumsy and experienced a strange icy feeling in her hands. She thought it must be her circulation but when the baby started to appear, she began to tremble and her teeth started to chatter. The midwife had an overwhelming sensation that something terrible was going to happen, experiencing what would now be labelled as a panic attack. She cut the cord and successfully delivered the child and, later, the sense of touch returned to her numb hands. However, for months afterwards she suffered terrible bouts of depression and even contemplated suicide. Why the midwife took such a strange turn is not known, but perhaps it was something to do with the fact that the new-born infant she had delivered was Adolf Hitler ...

Another example of a chilling premonition happened here in Liverpool. The case is known as the Harrington School Visions. At midday on 7 June 1926, Peter Kelly, a schoolboy, told a friend he had just seen something terrifying staring at him from a window in Harrington School, in Stanhope Street. Peter had almost fallen off his bicycle after seeing a grotesque skull gazing down at him from the school window. His mate was naturally sceptical and challenged Peter to show him what he had seen.

When the boys arrived at the school, a young woman was standing on the pavement, staring up at the windows of the building. She too had noticed the skull, which looked as if it was screaming. The boys also saw it and all around the apparition were leaping flames, which seemed to be consuming its grotesque face. The woman on the pavement screamed, threw her hands to her face and ran home to tell her family of the strange vision.

Crowds were soon swarming around the school, waiting for the vision to reappear. The thrill seekers were not to be disappointed and soon the ghostly face of an old woman materialised, wringing her hands and shaking her head. Superstitious members of the crowd made the sign of the cross and a gang of men who had been demolishing a house nearby, stopped work to see what was going on and witnessed a gallery of eerie faces in the windows. A man stared out with his hair on fire and in terrible pain before the flames scorched his face, turning it black, so that only his teeth and the whites of his eyes could be seen. The other faces were of children and, as the flames quickly obscured their heads, many in the crowd fainted or turned away in horror.

The fire brigade arrived, as people had assumed that there must be a fire raging inside, although there was no smoke coming from the building. When the firemen hammered on the school door, a janitor answered. He said he had just checked and there was no fire in the building.

The firemen went to the floor where the faces had been seen but found the classrooms deserted.

The *Liverpool Echo* and other newspapers reported the strange story claiming that it had been a case of mass hysteria and conjectured that the incident had probably been caused by reflections in the school windows. The janitor claimed he knew the truth but the journalists did not bother to interview him. The janitor knew that the glass panes, through which the burning faces had peered, had been salvaged from a house in Edge Hill. The house had been destroyed in a blaze which had claimed the lives of a large family. The helpless firefighters had witnessed the victims of the blaze, young and old, screaming at the windows as the smoke overcame them and the flames roasted them alive. An unscrupulous glazier later took many of the intact glass panes from the burnt-out house and used them in Harrington School. The janitor believed that the faces of the blaze victims had somehow been absorbed, or imprinted, on to the window panes. His theory was way ahead of its time, as this was years before holographic images could be stored on glass plates using a laser.

However, it seems that the Harrington School faces could also have been a premonition because, one year later, the janitor and his family were burnt alive when a fire broke out in their home. Witnesses of the blaze said he appeared at the window, desperately trying to open it, but the flames rose up and set fire to his hair. Within seconds, his face had turned black with the smoke and fire. The janitor, his four children, and his old mother, all died in the tragic blaze.

ANOTHER GIRL

At a semi-detached house in Tuebrook, in 1996, a young couple, Tony and Susan, were watching television one night, when, at a quarter to ten, the couple's little Jack Russell dog, Judy, padded in and looked at Susan, as if wanting to go out. Susan put on her sandals, grabbed her coat, and put Judy on a lead, then walked around the neighbourhood for about twenty minutes. When she returned to her house, she tip-toed through the front garden and spied on Tony through the living-room window, to see if he was having a sneaky cigarette – he had quit smoking for almost a week – but as she peered through the window, she was stunned by what she actually saw.

Sitting on the sofa was a red-haired young woman wearing nothing but a revealing negligee and black lacy underwear. The stranger was dipping a spoon into a small tub of ice cream as she watched the television, seemingly unaware of Susan. Susan's heart skipped a beat. Who was the girl? She certainly intended to find out and stormed to the front door and hammered on the knocker.

After almost a minute, Tony came downstairs complaining, "I was in the toilet! Don't tell me; you forgot your key again."

Susan pushed him roughly aside and let go of the dog's leash. She went into the living room demanding to know what was going on – but there was no girl there – just the television set blaring out to an empty living-room.

"What's up?" Tony asked, watching his girlfriend angrily snapping the curtains back, as if she was looking for someone.

Susan was naturally confused and told Tony about the

girl she had seen in their living room. Tony shook his head and laughed nervously.

"You must've been looking through next door's window. That girl next door, Stacey, she's got red hair."

"I looked through *this* window. This one! And the girl next door has brown hair and she's only fifteen. She was nothing like the girl I saw; her hair was red, and she looked about twenty-five."

Tony sat Susan down and hugged her, joking.

"Unless it was a ghost!"

"Don't be talking about things like that at this time of night," Susan shivered. "It was really weird. She looked so real. She was eating ice cream."

Next day, Tony went for a job interview at the Albert Dock as a barman at one of the pubs. Later that afternoon, Susan returned home from college and while she was making herself a cup of tea, she heard the gate outside clang shut. She assumed that it was Tony returning from his interview but, when she looked out of the window, she was astonished to see that it was the mysterious red-head she had seen sitting on her sofa. The woman was walking down the path towards the house. Susan braced herself.

That Tony has been seeing someone else. I knew it, she seethed. She waited tensely for the girl to knock but was shocked to hear a key rattle in the lock instead. The door opened and footsteps sounded on the stairs. Putting down her tea, Susan followed to confront her rival but the upstairs rooms were empty. Then something even more bizarre happened. Susan walked into the empty room where Tony stored all his football programmes and sports books, to find that the room had been transformed into a nursery and there was a baby crying in a cot in the corner.

She felt dizzy with shock.

At that moment, the front door opened and Tony shouted, "Sue! I got the job! I start Monday!"

Susan came downstairs but didn't give him the reception he had been hoping for.

"Whose is that baby upstairs?" she shrieked. "What the hell is going on?"

Tony followed her upstairs. When he looked into the box room, all that was to be seen were his old piles of books and football memorabilia. Susan put her hands to her face, "Tony, I think I should see a doctor. I'm sure I'm going mad. I saw a baby in a cot ... just there ... and that red-haired girl was here again. She came into the house."

A week later, Susan was alone in the house and went upstairs to the bathroom. Looking in the mirror, she noticed something flit past the doorway behind her. She only caught a fleeting glimpse, but she was sure it was the red-haired girl again. As she recovered from the fright, she heard an American voice coming from the bedroom saying, "Hi, Lauren! Mommy's come to change your diaper."

Susan heard a baby babbling and went into each room in turn but found them all empty.

Running downstairs, she telephoned the pub where Tony was working and begged him to come home at once. Shortly afterwards, Tony was sitting on the sofa with her, very concerned about her state of mind. Then he too heard something that defied rational explanation. A radio suddenly came on upstairs, even though Tony knew there was no radio upstairs. A rock song boomed out at full volume, followed by the voice of a girl with an American accent shouting, "Turn that down, Tony."

The song sounded as if it were being sung by the rock band, Oasis, but Tony, a fan of the group, had never heard it before. The sounds faded away and they went upstairs but there was no one about and no radio to be seen anywhere.

The biggest shock came the following Sunday morning. Susan came downstairs and smelt a strange, sweet aroma, the scent of flowers, emanating from the front room. Opening the door, she almost had a heart attack when she saw an open coffin on a stand, surrounded by wreaths and other floral tributes. In the coffin was her own body! She ran screaming up the stairs and threw herself at Tony. He began to tremble and tried to pacify her by saying that it had just been a bad dream but he, too, could smell the flowers. Yet when he went downstairs, he found the room empty.

A fortnight later, Susan was tragically knocked down and killed whilst visiting her cousin in Warrington. Before the funeral, her body was brought home and laid to rest in her coffin in the front room.

In November 1996, Tony met a red-haired American student who was staying in Britain. The girl is currently living with him, helping him to get over his loss. Recently, she discovered she was pregnant and the couple plan to call the baby Lauren, if it's a girl. Tony has already cleared out the boxroom and converted it into a nursery, just as Susan had foreseen a year before. When Tony heard that Oasis were bringing out a single, 'Stand By Me', he shuddered, recalling that that was the song he had heard blaring out from the upstairs radio. It was as if Tony and Susan had been seeing and hearing sneak previews of Tony's future life – with another girl.

PHANTOMS OF THE LIVING

According to recent research in the UK, Europe and the United States, a staggering forty-five per cent of all ghost sightings are actually encounters with phantasms of the living; phantom images of people who are in perfect health. Unlike the mysterious doppelganger – a sinister, solid-looking twin of a person who is often (supposedly) about to die – phantasms of a living person are short-lived and often seem ghost-like. Furthermore, these strange phantoms seemed to be unconsciously generated by the person in whose image they appear.

For centuries, occultists, mystics and magicians have claimed to be able to project three-dimensional images of themselves and there are old Hindu texts which claim that Krishna had the ability to multiply his likeness in flesh-and-blood form. But could the average person be capable of such an incredible feat? Much of the capacity of the human brain is under used and seems to be lying dormant most of the time. Could these areas be waiting in the wings for some future stage of human evolution, when the use of telepathy and other psychic talents will become the norm? Perhaps these under-used parts of the brain sometimes accidentally wake up before their time and temporarily give a sneak preview of the powers which the human race may one day possess. This theory would certainly throw some light on the following case of a projected phantom that was seen in Liverpool by three witnesses.

One January in the early 1990s, Angela, a nineteen-year-old Liverpool waitress, met Duncan, a twenty-year-old Glaswegian, at a Bold Street cafe. The couple got on really well and, on 29 February, Angela proposed to Duncan. It was a leap year and the traditional date for women to propose to their lovers. Duncan laughed at Angela's forwardness and agreed to marry her but, as he had hardly any money coming in from his job, said that she would have to wait a while for an engagement ring. Angela did not care; it was tongue-in-cheek anyway, their love surpassed any need for a ring.

Then Duncan received a letter from his brother in Glasgow, informing him that their mother was seriously ill. The doctors had diagnosed a brain tumour but did not yet know whether it was cancerous or benign. Duncan decided he would have to go back to Glasgow for a few days but Angela was unable to accompany him because she needed her job to pay the bills. The couple had one night out before Duncan returned to Scotland. They went to a club and, as they walked home, they started to kiss passionately, ending up embracing beneath an enormous iron statue in Concert Street. By coincidence, the statue – entitled 'Reconciliation' – was of two people embracing. Angela pleaded with Duncan to come back to Liverpool as soon as possible and then started to cry. Duncan brushed away her tears, promised that he would miss her, and said that she would be on his mind all the time.

The next day, Duncan left the city for his hometown. As she worked in the cafe, Angela kept thinking about her boyfriend and the things they had said to one another. She looked forward to getting a letter or phonecall from him.

A week went by and he still had not been in touch. Angela, feeling concerned, went to the Central Library and scoured the Glasgow phonebook, looking for Duncan's surname and address. She telephoned immediately and Duncan's brother, Alastair, answered and seemed very evasive about his brother's whereabouts. In the end, he admitted that Duncan was depressed about his mother's condition and was drowning his sorrows in the local pub with a former girlfriend.

In a state of numb shock, Angela managed to say, "Well, tell him to get in touch with me," before putting the phone down, and then walked all the way from William Brown Street to the Dingle, with a choking lump in her throat. "How could he do this to me?" she kept thinking.

Another week went by – the darkest week of her life. She could hardly eat and refused to go out with her friends. Each morning she would wait in vain for the postman, hoping against hope that Duncan had sent her a letter. Angela's two friends, Gina and Zoe, finally persuaded their broken-hearted girlfriend to go out with them. The three of them went to a club in Wood Street and had a great night. At 2.30 that morning, they were walking up Bold Street, singing and laughing, when they saw something that they would talk about for the rest of their lives.

The ghostly figure of a young man was standing at the base of the statue in Concert Street. He had his back turned to the girls, so they could not see his face. His head was bowed and his hands were resting on the statue. The girls halted in their tracks, because the figure was partially transparent. Gina swore and started to run shouting, "It's a ghost! It's a ghost!"

Zoe and Angela grabbed her and told her to calm down. They were more intrigued than frightened, but Angela almost fainted when the ghost slowly turned, because it was unmistakably the ghost of Duncan. He moved away from the statue and seemed to be crying.

Angela rushed in her high heels over to the ghostly figure shouting, "Duncan! It's me ... Angela."

But Duncan did not react and just faded away into thin air. The girls were so shocked and frightened that none of them remembered walking to Zoe's flat in Brownlow Hill. The three of them sat up all night, each going over their version of the strange incident.

A few days later, Duncan walked into the cafe in Bold Street where Angela worked and she almost dropped a tray of cups when she saw him standing there with a bunch of flowers. He explained that his mother had been operated on and that she was now well on the road to recovery, adding that the last weeks had been a living nightmare. He denied that he had been seeing his old flame. She had just provided platonic support for him in his hour of need, that was all.

Duncan then told a strange tale. He said that the previous Friday at 2.30am, he had been wandering the streets of Glasgow's city centre, when he came across an exact replica of the iron statue in Liverpool's Concert Street. Duncan had immediately thought of Angela and had hugged the statue, as he kept picturing himself in Liverpool with his girl.

At that exact moment, Angela and her friends had seen Duncan's figure at the base of the same statue off Bold Street. Angela and Duncan had not been aware that there were three copies of the statue in Concert Street which were unveiled in Belfast, Glasgow and Liverpool at the same time, as a symbolic gesture of peace, in 1990.

RAMBLING ROSE

The following story has been vouched for by many people over the years and concerns a particularly gruesome apparition. Let me warn you now; if you are a security guard in the Liverpool area, look out for Rose; because you have a very good chance of seeing her ... maybe even tonight.

The alarming apparition was first seen in the mid-1970s at a certain premises which security guards patrolled into the small hours. In 1975, a new guard, Trevor, was walking down the corridors of this building. He was a bit nervous and kept wondering what he would do if intruders actually got into the building he was supposed to be guarding.

"What if they were armed?" he thought, anxiously, as he turned a corner.

For some unfathomable reason, he expected to find someone standing there. In his mind's eye he had caught a glimpse of a woman with her arms outstretched towards him. He remembers thinking how strange it was to receive such an unusually vivid mental impression. Then Trevor felt an icy sensation creeping up his spine. He just knew there was something behind him and was gripped with fear. He gulped and made himself carry on walking, afraid to turn around but, as he reached the door ahead, he saw the reflection of the thing behind him – a naked woman with long matted hair and a skeletal face – reaching out towards him. Trevor flung the door open and ran as fast as his legs could carry him up the stairs to the next floor, to where his colleague, Brian, was patrolling.

"Brian! I just saw the ghost," shouted Trevor. "It was horrible, really horrible!"

"Don't be so da ..." responded Brian, his jaw dropping

as he too saw the apparition. He let out a terrible scream and made a scramble for an empty storeroom, with Trevor in hot pursuit.

"Switch the light on!" Trevor yelled, as Brian fumbled for the switch. The feeble 40-watt light in its dusty shade allowed them to see the handle of the door turn twice.

Trevor panicked and screamed a string of four-letter obscenities at the thing on the other side of the door. Then there was a long silence. The guards could hear the door in the other room closing but they did not venture out of the room until six o'clock in the morning.

"Was it that thing you were talking about the other night?" Trevor asked, recalling the ghost story Brian had insisted on telling him.

Brian nodded, "Yeah ... Rose. The other fellow used to call her that after that old song, 'Ramblin' Rose'."

"I think I'll hand me cards in ... I'm not staying on here."

"Oh nice one, leave me here on me own," stammered Brian, still shaking from the encounter.

"It was so solid ... What does the one you're talking about look like, Brian?"

"It's a woman. She's in the nude but she's got parts of her skin missing ... like she's been cut up. She's got no skin on her face, just all exposed muscle and bone. Her eyeballs are the worst. One of them looked like it had burst, like a squashed tomato. The other one just stares ... no lids. Her jaw kept on opening, as if she was trying to get her words out. Ugh! She's not a pretty sight."

"Why don't we go and get a job somewhere else?" suggested Trevor. "There's no need to put up with this."

Brian nodded, "I think you're right. I've been here nine months and I thought all the stories about Ramblin' Rose were just a load of old rubbish but about a month back, I kept on finding lights switched back on. Then I heard footsteps in the corridor and started seeing something out the corner of me eye. Now I know why they pay so much per hour. See, she makes one big appearance like earlier on, then she might not appear again for weeks. The last fellow who was here said she didn't appear for six months once."

"Forget all that, Brian, we'll tell the boss to shove the job," Trevor insisted.

"The money's good though, Trev, that's the only thing. I'm up to me eyeballs in debt and Maureen'd kill me if I just packed the job in. Shall we just try and stick it one more night and see what happens?" Brian suggested.

"No way! I'm not staying in this place again tonight," Trevor said, shaking his head, as he mentally relived the frightening experience.

"Look, if she does put in an appearance, I swear that I'll leave the building with you straight away. How's that?" Brian offered.

Trevor grumbled but, as it was getting light outside, the young guard was beginning to feel slightly more confident.

"What do you say, then?" Brian asked. "They reckon the dead can't hurt you; it's the living that harms … Just one more night?"

Trevor reluctantly agreed. The next morning at 3am, the guards patrolled the building together, with their torches, even though all the lights were on.

"Isn't it funny how the place isn't as scary as we imagined it to be yesterday morning?" Brian said.

Trevor smiled weakly, "Hey, wouldn't it be funny if this Ramblin' Rose was just a cleaner trying to scare us?"

"That wasn't a cleaner the other morning, Trev."

"Let's stay off the subject. Stop talking about the flippin' supernatural, will you?"

The two started to chat about football instead and they soon felt confident enough to patrol the building on their own and Trevor even shouted out, "Come out, Ramblin' Rose! Matt Monroe wants you. Ha ha!"

Brian shouted after him, "And you were the one going to pack the job in!" Which made them both laugh.

Trevor then went down to the toilet and Brian decided to play a joke on him. He would sneak in and tap on the toilet door.

He tiptoed in and bent down to look under each of the cubicles to find which one Trevor was in. To his horror, he saw that under one of the doors there were *four* feet: Trevor's Doc Martens and two yellowed, fungus-ravaged, bare feet with blackened toe-nails. Brian fled straight out of the toilet and then out of the building. Returning with two bemused policemen, they found Trevor slumped on the toilet, unconscious: his face twitching as if he was having a seizure. When he regained consciousness in hospital, he told a doctor that he had been in the toilet when he had suddenly seen the most hideous figure of a woman appearing before him. Then he must have fainted.

Trevor and Brian both packed in the security guard job that same day. The ghost was then dormant for a few years, but appeared irregularly throughout the 1980s and is now said to be on the prowl once again. Three separate mediums have been called in by the management of the building to determine whose phantom it is and all three agreed it was the unquiet spirit of a young woman who had died in the 1950s, having donated her body to medical science.

However, it appears that she was not actually dead but in a cataleptic coma, which was mistaken for death, when her body was handed over to the laboratory. A student, who was stripping away the cadaver's skin with a scalpel, panicked when it began to twitch and then screamed. He reached for its throat and stabbed it repeatedly in the heart and neck with the scalpel.

Weeks later, after the body had been cut up into sections, which were then dissected yet again by students, it was 'buried' rather irreverently at a certain refuse site. This site was beneath the building where Ramblin' Rose roams the corridors …

MY VICTORIAN FATHER

This is one of the most bizarre stories I have ever come across and I first heard it from a perfectly level-headed listener, who contacted me after hearing one of my other stories on the radio.

Roger was a twenty-seven-year-old sales assistant, working in an art shop on Renshaw Street, in 1965. One day, Richard, a local artist, came into the store and bought a large canvas and a couple of paintbrushes. He got chatting to Roger, saying he would make an ideal model for his current project, because of his height and interesting profile. Roger was reassured that he would only be asked to pose fully-clothed and, what was more, he would be paid, even though it would only be a "few bob".

Roger agreed and the artist gave him the address of his Huskisson Street studio, asking him to call there at eight the following evening. When Roger turned up, a young girl opened the door. She was very beautiful but was dressed quite dowdily in a black polo-neck sweater and a long pleated dark-brown dress.

"You must be Roger. My name's Virginia," she announced rather self-consciously.

Roger accompanied the girl up the stairs to an attic studio under the eaves of the house. The place was like an explosion in a paint factory and the combined aroma of turps and varnish was overpowering. Richard put down his palette and posed Roger in a chair with his legs crossed in a casual manner and started to sketch him. Virginia just looked on, smiling at the subject. By about 11 o'clock, Richard decided he had done enough and showed Roger his work. It was a fairly detailed drawing for a preliminary sketch, but still needed a lot more work doing to it. Richard paid his new subject in cash and asked him to come back the next day at the same time. Virginia escorted Roger down the flights of stairs and they left the flat together. Roger asked her where she lived and offered to walk her home.

She said she lived in Mount Street, adding, "I appreciate your offer, but I must desist. You don't know what father is like, Roger. He simply does not allow me to become involved with men."

"That's a bit strict isn't it?" Roger laughed. "You're only young and you have got a life to live."

Virginia started to sniffle and shake, "I should have been back home at 9 o'clock. He will beat me now."

"No, he won't," said Roger, "Virginia, you're coming for a drink with me," he said, and took the girl to a local pub called Ye Cracke.

Virginia looked like a frightened rabbit and looked nervously about at the other drinkers. She told Roger she had never been inside a pub before and had never tasted alcohol. Roger said she should make up for lost time and plied her with another drink. When they left, the girl was pretty drunk and began to cry, saying her father would beat her senseless when she got home. Suddenly, a tall man wearing a short cape and a deerstalker hat came marching down Hope Street, ostentatiously swinging a cane as he strutted along.

"That's him," cried Virginia, cringing. "That's my father! He'll kill me!"

Roger quickly ushered her into the shadows of a nearby doorway and watched as the antiquated-looking man marched past. As he passed the young couple, they heard him mutter under his breath, "Where can she be? What the deuce has happened to the girl?" And he took a gold watch on a chain from his waistcoat and inspected it before walking on into the night, still muttering angrily to himself.

Roger escorted Virginia to his basement flat near Catherine Street. He said he would sleep on the sofa and offered Virginia his bed but she asked him to sleep with her. Roger was taken aback when she stripped to her underwear, climbed into the bed and begged him to get in with her. He did not need a second invitation, however, and was soon caressing her but they could not make love because she was wearing a great iron chastity belt of some sort. Virginia was ashamed and admitted that her father had the only key and had fitted the belt to prevent her from losing her virginity.

Her father, she said, claimed to be fifty-five but an old woman in the street had told her she had been an admirer of his when they were both twenty. That woman was now in her nineties! One day, when Virginia was rooting through her father's room while he was out of the house, she had found an old sepia-toned picture of him wearing a top hat. The caption on the photograph read, 'Birkenhead, 1892'.

"Perhaps it was his father, or grandfather," Roger suggested. "Sons and fathers can look alike."

But Virginia pointed out the man in the old photo had a mole on his left cheek, just like her father.

"What's your father's name?" Roger asked, his curiosity aroused.

"It's Robert Jones," replied Virginia and then told Roger about the collection of wedding photographs, with dates ranging from 1895 to 1945, that she had also found in the same drawer.

"He has been married seven times," Virginia said. "He married my mother just after the War. I think he's a devil, Roger … seriously … it's as if he's always been alive."

"Don't be so silly," laughed Roger, but Virginia's story was starting to give him the creeps. "He certainly acts like a Victorian; making you wear a chastity belt, for goodness sake. You've got to go to the police in the morning. I'll go with you, if you like. This is 1965 – not the Dark Ages," and he fell asleep embracing her.

When he awoke in the morning, Virginia was nowhere to be seen. Roger went to Richard's studio in Huskisson Street and told him about Virginia and her creepy father. Richard agreed that he had always thought there was something weird about him but had no idea that he had been cruel enough to make his daughter wear a chastity belt. He gave Roger the girl's address in Mount Street, but when Roger called, the house was unoccupied. The neighbours did not know where Mr Jones and his daughter had moved to and described him as an eccentric, reclusive man, who used to stroll down the street angrily pointing his walking cane at the television aerials, saying to anyone who would listen, that he would never allow a television in his home because they were immoral.

Roger never saw Virginia again, but it was not the end of the story.

In the severe winter of 1980, Roger – now aged forty-two – was driving near Upper Parliament Street through a blizzard. He stopped at the traffic lights and happened to glance at the taxi to his right. The passenger was talking to a woman and pointing at the falling snowflakes. Roger suddenly recognised the man. It was Robert Jones, Virginia's old-fashioned father. Roger realised, to his utter astonishment, that he had not changed one iota in the fifteen years that had elapsed since he had last seen him – and he was still wearing that deerstalker hat. Roger tried to follow the taxi but lost sight of it near Smithdown Road.

The mystery of Robert Jones haunted Roger for some time. Then, a few years later, he heard a local radio news story about how workmen in Duke Street had accidentally drilled into a crumbling family vault on the edge of St James's Cemetery. According to the inscription on the vault door, the coffin of a Victorian surgeon, Robert Jones, was buried within. Roger was flabbergasted to discover that the vault contained three other coffins belonging to the Jones family but that the coffin containing Robert Jones was missing. The report concluded that the missing coffin had probably sunk through the floor of the vault as a result of subsidence but, to Roger, only one bizarre explanation fitted the facts; and that was that the sinister Robert Jones had never actually died after all … and perhaps he is still alive to this day.

WHISPERS FROM A DEATH MASK

In January 1922, twenty-four-year-old auburn-haired Maggie, came out of the Vines public house, which still stands on the corner of Lime Street and Copperas Hill. She had arranged to meet Rex, a young man who worked in a nearby hotel, but there was no sign of him as yet. Maggie was shivering in the icy wind that blew down Lime Street, when a voice behind her asked, "Looking for someone, miss?" Maggie spun round to face a small man, about five feet three inches tall, standing there with a childish grin on his face. The man looked shabby and had three day old stubble on his chin.

"Yes, I'm waiting for my boyfriend. He said he'd be here at eight o'clock," Maggie replied, glancing up and down the street once more.

"What's your boyfriend like?" the stranger inquired.

"He's got blond hair and he's quite tall."

"There's a fellow of that description talking to a man around the corner."

"Really?" said Maggie and peered up Copperas Hill.

"I'll show you where he is, if you like," offered the man, and without waiting for an answer, led Maggie by the wrist along the street towards a narrow lane that used to stand near Bolton Street. As he reached the dimly-lit lane, his child-like expression changed and he produced a small clasp knife and held it against Maggie's delicate neck.

"Don't scream, or I'll cut your throat!" he said with a horrible grimace.

He shoved her into an alleyway and committed a serious sexual assault, throughout which he ground his teeth loudly. Finally, he punched her and sent her flying on to a stack of wooden crates at the back of the pub.

After the attack, the police stepped up patrols in the area but, for a fortnight, there were no further attacks reported. Then, on the night of 24 January, a small, middle-aged man seized a prostitute in Lord Nelson Street and, after an unsuccessful rape attempt, stole her earrings and purse before running off, laughing in a high-pitched voice as he went. Again, the police were unable to catch him. Three days later, there were two more attacks on women in Liverpool, one in Cropper Street, where a policeman gave chase to the rapist before he could assault the woman and the other, a mere forty-five minutes later, in the very alley off Copperas Hill where he had first struck. During this assault, the man ground his teeth and then bit the twenty-one-year-old victim's shoulder. He then ripped off a gold chain and locket and made his escape.

The police had no inkling as to who the offender was, until an old lady walked into Cheapside Bridewell and reported that she had seen a small man with evil, shifty-looking eyes on many occasions. She was sure he was the rapist because he was ogling at the legs of all the young women walking up Lime Street. The police sent out plain clothes detectives to patrol the street and, within hours, the little man appeared, giving himself away by leering at every woman who passed. The detectives followed him as he walked down Lime Street and then stopped to take out a bunch of keys to unlock the door of one of Liverpool's famous attractions, Reynold's Waxworks.

The police grabbed the man, Alfie Begg, a fifty-seven-year-old bachelor, who lived with his mother and worked as a temporary watchman at the wax museum. As the detectives escorted Begg into the waxworks, in handcuffs, he began to cry, repeatedly declaring "I'm innocent of these crimes. It's all Deeming's doing."

"Deeming? Who's he?" one of the detectives asked.

It was extremely eerie down in the Chamber of Horrors. There was a clockwork-driven model of Marie Antoinette being guillotined and numerous graphic torture scenes in a realistic mock-up of the Inquisition. What was even more gruesome, was the line-up of life-like heads of famous murderers from the 1840s to the present day. All the heads were actual plaster cast impressions, taken from the killers after they had been hanged. One of these death masks belonged to one of the most notorious mass-murderers of all time, Frederick Deeming, the Birkenhead-born psychopath who had killed every member of his own family and then danced on their graves with his next victim.

Mr Begg pointed his handcuffed hands at the head of the killer and announced, "Meet Mr Deeming!"

The detectives looked at each other and shook their heads. The nightwatchman was obviously seriously mentally deranged.

Begg then addressed the death mask, "Say hello to our visitors, Mr Deeming."

One of the detectives smirked: "He's not saying anything till he sees his solicitor, eh?"

Then a squeaky trembling voice said, "I hate coppers."

The detectives were naturally startled by the sound and looked about the other gruesome wax effigies, expecting to see someone lurking in the shadows, but there was no one else about.

"You'd better come with us, Mr Begg," said a policeman, feeling a bit edgy, and hoping that Begg had a talent for ventriloquism!

"If I promise not to hurt any women again, will you leave me alone please?" Mr Begg pleaded, again adopting his childish persona.

"Come along, sir," said one of the detectives, escorting him away from the rogue's gallery. "Let's get you to the station."

Begg started to cry and turned back to the death-mask of Frederick Deeming saying, "They're taking me away and it's all your fault, Mr Deeming! You made me do it!"

At the bridewell, Begg repeated that he was just a simple man who had been driven to crime because the murderer, Deeming, had forced him into carrying out the rapes and robberies. The clasp knife he had used was not his, but had been taken from one of the waxwork exhibits. Several people who had known Alfie Begg testified that the man was a stable, if somewhat slow person, definitely not known for the quickness of his mind. He had no criminal record and had once been praised for rescuing a dog from a frozen lake in Sefton Park. When a psychiatrist asked him about his conversations with the sinister talking head, Alfie Begg replied, "Mr Deeming's spirit said it was really scared because the Devil had found out that he had been hiding in his death mask for years."

The psychiatrist chuckled, "What will the Devil do to poor Mr Deeming's spirit, now that he's found him?"

Alfie Begg looked worried, "Mr Deeming said that Satan would claw his spirit back to Hell," adding, "I saw Satan once. He came up, out of the ground, in the Chamber of Horrors. I was really scared."

"What did the Devil look like, Alfie?" coaxed the psychiatrist.

"Bloomin' horrible. I had nightmares afterwards. Satan is like a tall dark-haired man but he was surrounded by flames. All these terrible screaming voices were all around him. He said they were the damned – bad people who were trapped in Hell."

The psychiatrist scribbled Alfie's words down, dismissing him as a schizophrenic. Then Alfie held out his left hand and pointed to his wrist. There was a thick straight scar right across it.

"The Devil touched me there and burned me. I cried and he laughed. He said he'd be back one day for Deeming and that he'd burn the place down."

Later that week, the police psychiatrist was astounded to learn that Reynold's Wax Museum had been gutted by a fire of unknown origin. The psychiatrist visited the ruin of the waxworks and a fire officer took him down the steps to what remained of the Chamber of Horrors. In the grotesque mass of melted figures was one exhibit that had almost survived the previous night's mysterious inferno – the distorted head of Frederick Deeming. The heat had partially melted the head and its jaws had buckled open, making Deeming appear to be crying out in agony. The psychiatrist and the fire officer were leaving the burnt-out shell when a faint voice cried out, "Help me, Jesus!" They turned around but there was no one about.

Stranger still, when the psychiatrist visited Alfie Begg in a mental institution later that week and told him about the fire and Deeming's partially melted death mask, Begg replied, "I know! Mr Deeming told me. He was here last night, you see. Then the Devil dragged him off to Hell."

THE FACE AT THE WINDOW

One of the oddest and most baffling phenomena of the 1960s and 1970s was the huge revival of mysticism and the occult. The man who was single-handedly responsible for reviving the worldwide interest in witchcraft was Gerald Gardner, who was born at Great Crosby in 1884.

Britain has a long history of witches and warlocks – from the Druids of thousands of years ago to the Pendle Hill witches. Officially, black magic was banned in Britain under the Witchcraft Act of 1753. This act was replaced in 1951 by the Fraudulent Mediums Act but, surely, no one believes in witches in today's high-tech world? I have to tell you that, on the contrary, witches are still very much around. In fact, there is probably a local coven in your area.

In the summer of 1979, George Sidwell and Andrea King from Edge Hill, went on a day trip to Blackpool, spending a small fortune on the fair. Before heading home, Andrea saw a sign: 'Enter and Petra will look into your future. A genuine psychic of Romany descent'.

"Ooh! Look, George, a fortune teller. Let's go and have our fortunes told."

George was superstitious and not keen on having his fortune read but Andrea persuaded him that it was only a bit of harmless fun.

They entered the dimly-lit room, where an old, white-haired woman was sitting at a table in the middle of which was a crystal ball on a stand. It all appeared rather corny to George, like something out of a kid's story book, but Andrea was completely taken in and thought it was very exciting. The gypsy introduced herself as Petra and asked for three pounds in advance.

George begrudgingly handed over the money, which she grabbed and stashed away in her belt. She then gazed into the ball for what seemed like a very long time. George was just going to demand his money back, when Petra's eyes suddenly widened with alarm. Turning to Andrea she announced, "Someone has the evil eye on you."

"What?" asked Andrea.

"The evil eye. It's a woman. You don't know her but she knows you. She wants something that you've got."

Petra rubbed her eyes, she seemed to be finding it hard to concentrate.

"What's the evil eye? What are you talking about?" Andrea asked.

George grabbed her hand, "I told you this was a bad idea. It's a load of old rubbish. Come on, let's go."

But Andrea would not budge. She had to know more.

"What else can you see?" she asked anxiously.

"Another three pounds first, please," demanded Petra.

George was flabbergasted at the woman's effrontery: "Another three quid? No way, Gypsy Lee! Let's go, love."

George tugged at Andrea but she stayed firmly where she was and said: "Don't spoil what's been a nice day out, George. Just give her the three pounds."

George let go of her hand in a huff and shoved another three pounds across the table, muttering, "This had better be good!"

Petra gazed back into the crystal globe. After a while, she suddenly said, "Hear my advice. Move to another house, as far away from Liverpool as you can go."

"Is that it?" George said, shaking his head.

Petra took out a black velvet cloth and covered the crystal ball marking the end of the session.

"That is all there is," she said, looking drained and fatigued.

George dragged Andrea out of the tent and the couple

then argued all the way back to their Liverpool home, a seventh-storey flat in Entwistle Heights, a high-rise block of apartments. Two nights later, George was sound asleep in bed, while Andrea was reading a book beside him. At exactly 1.45am, she glanced at the window and saw a face looking in at her. She screamed and shook George awake, pointing to the window – but by the time he had fully woken up, the face had disappeared. Andrea explained what she had seen but George just laughed, "Andrea, we're seven storeys up, for goodness sake. How could anyone peep in at you? Unless it was Spiderman, of course! You've been dreaming, that's all."

Andrea slept uneasily that night, held in George's embrace. At 4.00am, she opened her eyes only to find that the face was at the window again: the face of a woman grinning in at her. Andrea pinched George's arm hard and he awoke with a cry of pain.

"What's up with you tonight?" he asked, exasperated.

The face had vanished again, so she did not tell George and began to fear for her own state of mind.

"Sorry, love. I must have grabbed you in my sleep."

Two days later, Andrea decided to visit a hairdressers downtown. About thirty minutes into getting her hair done, she looked up and saw the reflection of a woman in a long black dress in the mirror. The woman's face was unnaturally pale and she wore rather a lot of black eyeliner; making her appear even more sinister. Andrea immediately recognised the face – it was the same face that had been looking into her flat two days back. Suddenly, in the blink of an eye, the woman vanished. Andrea let out a scream, startling the hairdresser, who had seen nothing strange.

Andrea then visited a Mrs Coombes, a spiritualist who had been recommended to her by a friend. When she told her about the supernatural woman who was stalking her, the medium instantly became alarmed and said: "Oh, I don't want to get involved with that sort of thing, dear. It's over my head! I'm sorry but you must leave!" She began to tremble visibly and quickly showed Andrea the door. Andrea was a nervous wreck by now. What had she said that had frightened the medium off? Weren't they supposed to be able to deal with that sort of thing?

The next alarming encounter with the solid-looking phantom was in the most unexpected and almost comical location. Andrea was soaking in the bath on the following Sunday evening, catching up with Saturday's *Echo*, when she happened to glance over the top of the newspaper – and there was the creepy woman in black, sitting on the toilet seat as large as life, grinning at her. Andrea instinctively screamed and threw the newspaper at the apparition, which vanished instantly.

Andrea was becoming mentally and physically exhausted and was so paranoid that she looked at every female figure she came across with suspicion. She kept glancing at the windows in the flat every few seconds, expecting the woman to spring out at her every time she entered a room. George suggested that she see a psychiatrist, but Andrea insisted that she was not imagining things. Her odd behaviour soon proved too much of a strain on George and he left her a week later, without leaving a forwarding address. Andrea was devastated and yet, for some strange reason, she never saw the apparition while she was alone in the flat.

A fortnight later, she went to town to buy herself a dress and decided to walk back home as it was a sunny day. As she passed Abercromby Square, she noticed George sprawled out on the grass, soaking up the sun, with a woman in sunglassses, lying beside him, holding his hand. Andrea's heart broke in two there and then. The proud part of her just wanted to walk on by but instead she remained rooted to the spot. She then found herself storming into the park to confront her ex-boyfriend and his new girlfriend.

"George!" she shouted.

George and his girlfriend looked up at Andrea, startled.

"Andrea!" said George, seemingly stuck for words.

"It didn't take you long to find someone else did it? She's a bit old for you though, isn't she, George?" Andrea said, sneering at the woman, who looked about ten to fifteen years older than George. "Unless she's your mum, of course."

The woman next to George took off her sunglasses. It was none other than the weirdo who had recently been haunting Andrea and almost given her a nervous breakdown – the face at the window – the apparition that had followed her everywhere. Her stomach turned over.

"You!" she gasped.

"Yes … me … Satisfied? Now go away, or else!"

"Or else what?" Andrea demanded, trying to put on a brave face.

The woman suddenly pointed over to a man leaving the park and whispered something unintelligible under her breath. Without warning, the man collapsed on to the pavement. People rushed to his aid but he was already dead, as if his heart had simply given out.

The woman who had seemingly caused the accident then pointed accusingly at Andrea, "Impressed? Now walk away. That's right. Go on."

Then something chilling happened. As she was turning round, almost against her will, she heard George say, "Don't Andrea! Please don't leave me."

But Andrea kept walking and did not stop until she was back home.

She never saw George or the mysterious woman again. To this day, Andrea believes that her boyfriend was not swept off his feet by a domineering older woman, but was forcibly taken from her by a modern day witch. The police were reluctant to get involved when she told them about the abduction and it was obvious that they felt that her mind had been turned by her partner's desertion. All the same, George Sidwell was subsequently put on the missing persons register – but he still has not been traced.

THE CALLER

This creepy incident took place in Liverpool in 1995. In December of that year, a Jewish family moved into an Edwardian house in Aigburth, just as Karen, the youngest of the family, had turned fifteen. She was a very pretty girl who was often asked out on dates but she had her eye on a boy called Damon, who lived close to her new home. She often used to meet him and chat as they walked their dogs in the local park.

One night, Karen dialled directory enquiries and asked for Damon's telephone number. She then dialled the number but got an engaged tone. She tried again ten minutes later but the line was still busy. Karen wondered if Damon was chatting on the phone with some girl and, with that depressing thought in her head, she hung up and decided to try and read a romantic novel in bed.

The phone rang later that night and Karen's father answered it. He shouted up to his daughter's bedroom, "Karen, you're wanted on the phone!"

Karen rushed downstairs and grabbed the receiver.

A boy's voice said, "Hello."

"Hi, who are you?"

"Jason. Is that Sarah?"

"I'm afraid you've got the wrong number," said Karen and was ready to hang up.

Then the boy said, "I'm sorry about that, but hey, what's your name?"

"Why?" asked Karen suspiciously, yet at the same time excited at the thought of talking to a strange boy.

"You know my name. So what's yours?" said Jason with a laugh in his voice.

"It's Karen, if you must know. Okay? Now goodbye," said Karen, pretending she was about to hang up.

"No, wait!" Jason pleaded. "Don't go, Karen, what do you look like? I know this sounds dead corny but I imagine you as a tall girl with big blue eyes and long black hair."

Karen blushed as if Jason was standing in front of her. She gave a little nervous laugh and her heart fluttered.

"Why are you laughing? Do you think I've been spying on you?" said Jason. "Because I'm right, aren't I? You are tall with long dark hair."

Karen bit her lip. "Hundreds of girls have black hair and blue eyes. Anyway, hadn't you better go and ring Sarah? I take it she's your girlfriend?"

"Not any more," said Jason, gloomily.

"Why not?"

"We just lost touch. I moved away from the area you see, but I've moved back now."

"Who are you talking to?" interrupted Karen's father. He liked to keep a close eye on his daughter where boys were concerned.

"Nobody," she replied and glared at him for being so interfering.

"Was that your dad?" Jason asked.

— 156 —

"Yeah. So, Jason, are you going to get back with Sarah if you can?"

"No, not now. It's been too long. She's probably with someone else by now. Listen, why don't we meet up somewhere?"

"What? Meet? Oh, I'm not sure. I don't really know you!" said Karen, twisting the telephone flex round her fingers.

"Go on, it would be a laugh," Jason insisted.

"Karen, who *is* that on the phone?" her father asked.

"A friend … okay?" Karen snapped.

"Yes, but who is this friend?"

"His name's Jason! Can't I talk to my own friends without you asking me twenty questions every time?"

"Don't talk to me like that!" Karen's father warned his insolent daughter.

Jason laughed, "Wow! You can't half answer back. My parents used to hit me when I gave cheek like that."

To get back at her parents, Karen suddenly decided that she would meet this Jason after all.

"Okay, I'll meet you someplace. How about McDonald's?"

"Which one?" asked Jason, startled and surprised.

"You know, on the corner of Church Street and Paradise Street," said Karen, in a deliberately loud voice.

The girl's parents looked on, outraged at her boldness.

"Okay, McDonald's it is then. What time?"

"After school; between four fifteen and four thirty. How will we recognise each other?"

"I'll be wearing a blue T-shirt and I've got blond curly hair. I'll wait for you outside, near the entrance. Anyway, I'll know you, because you're tall with long black hair, aren't you?" he laughed.

"I'm not that tall – about five seven. Anyway, see you tomorrow then."

Karen hung up and flounced past her parents and up to her room, feeling excited but a little worried about the bizarre blind date.

The following day, she arrived at McDonald's at ten past four but there was no sign of Jason. She waited for what she considered a reasonable time, but he didn't turn up. He telephoned that night to say that he had got cold feet and had bottled out at the last minute. So another romantic rendezvous was arranged, again at McDonald's, but Jason did not show up again. This time, his excuse was that he had been detained at school for messing about in class. Karen did not believe him and asked which school he went to. He told her that he went to Nugent High School in Edge Hill. When Karen told her mum, she said that that was strange, because her friend's son had been a pupil at the Nugent High School and it had been demolished years ago.

When Jason rang again, Karen accused him of being a liar and he hung up after saying, "I love you, Karen, and you don't know why I'm shy."

Karen felt guilty about accusing her new friend of lying and when he rang again, she changed her tone slightly and said, "Look, Jason, I really like you. I don't know why you don't want to meet me, but if you're worried I might think you're spotty, or too small, or too ugly, I swear I'll still like you. I can tell you've got a boss personality and I think … oh … nothing."

"You think what?" asked Jason.

Karen looked around and waited until her mum had gone into the kitchen, then whispered: "I think I love you. Now do you believe me?"

"I love you too," Jason said and started to cry.

"Don't cry," Karen said, "I don't care what you look like.

We'll meet tonight, okay? You can come round to my house – we'll watch a video or something."

She gave him her address and he promised that he would arrive at seven that evening, but seven o'clock came and went and there was no sign of the boy.

At 9.00pm, the phone rang and Karen dashed to answer it. It was Jason and he finally dropped the bombshell.

"You won't be hearing from me again, Karen," he stammered, his voice breaking up.

"Don't be stupid," Karen said, and then asked him why he had not turned up again.

"You really want to know the truth?" Jason sobbed.

"Yes, get it off your chest. Tell me why you can't, or won't face me?" Karen demanded, desperate to know what could possibly be the problem.

"I've been ... dead ... for five years. Yes ... dead!" Jason screamed and the line went silent – deathly silent.

That was the last Karen ever heard from the boy. Her mother got in touch with a psychic research group and they claimed that a boy named Jason had lived in Karen's Aigburth home five years before. Jason had dropped dead while playing football outside in the street, because he had something wrong with his heart. Was this the same Jason who had developed such a crush on Karen? The psychic investigators thought it highly likely, because they discovered that Jason had had curly blond hair and that he had been dating a girl named Sarah before his untimely death. Even now, whenever the phone rings, Karen still jumps – just in case it's him.

THE CLOCK-WATCHER

In 1958, postal worker George Jones, was out shopping with his wife, Claire, an incurable shopaholic, in Liverpool's Lime Street. Claire came to a stop in front of a jeweller's window and gazed dreamily, and meaningfully, at the array of rings and necklaces in their tempting crimson velvet-lined trays.

"Look, don't start, love," moaned George.

"Ooh, isn't that ring beautiful?" sighed Claire, wistfully, ignoring her husband and pointing to a gold ring set with a single iridescent sapphire.

"I'm a postman, not Rockefeller," George grumbled.

Claire ignored the remark and entered the jeweller's and George rolled his eyes and reluctantly trailed after her.

"Ooh! Isn't that a gorgeous clock, George?" remarked Claire. "Wouldn't it look great on our mantelpiece in the front room? I can just see it!"

She had spotted an unusual timepiece mounted in a glass case on the top shelf. The clock had a beautiful dark blue enamel finish and an intricate stand made of cream-coloured porcelain. The clockface was framed with a golden circular band and the hours were inscribed in Roman numerals.

George looked up at the clock, then turned to the jeweller, an old grey-haired man. In a resigned voice, he asked the price.

"Twenty pounds," the jeweller replied, as his wife suddenly appeared from the back of the shop, wringing her hands anxiously.

"Oh, we've got to have it at that price, George," Claire said, tugging her husband's arm.

George realised that Claire had forgotten about the expensive-looking sapphire ring in the window, so, with a smug look, he took out his wallet and counted out the twenty pounds in notes.

"If it makes you happy, love," George said, handing the money to the jeweller.

The jeweller's wife could barely contain her joy at the sale and George surmised that business was slow and assumed that that was why the jeweller and his wife were so excited by the sale. The jeweller wrote out a receipt and then fetched a small step ladder in order to reach the clock. He laid it on the counter and his wife brought a cardboard box from the back room with straw and newspaper to package the timepiece.

At this point, Claire's attention was caught by an unusual feature on the clock that she hadn't noticed before. A little black enamelled devil was sitting on the top of the glass case. The horned devil was slumped forward, as if he had nodded off, and in his hand he clutched the typical three-pronged fork which is usually associated with the Devil. Claire thought the little devil was rather cute, with his tiny pointed tail and little red cloak.

"George, look, the little devil's head moves," said Claire excitedly, suddenly noticing that the little figure's head was nodding slightly.

The jeweller laughed nervously: "That's right, madam. It's the pendulum action you see. He's supposed to be the devil having a sleep. He's nodded off, so all the evil in the world has stopped. But when the clock stops, he springs up and opens his eyes. His eyes are two tiny little green emeralds. It's intriguing, isn't it?"

"Bloody weird, if you ask me," muttered George.

"A French clockmaker made a limited number of these.

A Monsieur Fericul of Rouen. So this timepiece is a real investment, provided you look after it properly."

That afternoon, at her home in Muirhead Avenue, Claire placed the new clock on the mantelpiece and invited her neighbours round to show it off. However, she had forgotten to wind it up and slowly, the sleeping devil on top of the clock started lifting and dropping his head, as if he was ready to wake at any moment.

Claire's next door neighbours were two old spinsters, Lily and Nellie. They sat at the table in the living room, sipping tea and nibbling sandwiches, as they eyed the novelty clock with unbridled jealousy.

"It looks a bit funny where you've put it, Claire. Whatever made you buy it?" asked Nellie, smirking at Lily.

Lily carried her cup and saucer over to the mantelpiece, the better to inspect the clock. She stroked the little slumbering devil and asked, "What's this supposed to be, Claire? Is it a devil?"

At that moment, a strange silence fell on the room. The clock had stopped ticking. The devil on top of it looked up and his eyelids popped open, revealing a pair of exceedingly sinister-looking emerald eyes. It took Lily by surprise and she dropped the cup and saucer, which both smashed on the hearth tiles.

"Lily! You butterfingers!" said Nellie.

Then Lily collapsed. As she fell, her head hit the edge of the stone mantelpiece, knocking out several of her front teeth. She lay there, shaking violently, her body racked with terrible spasms. Her face was contorted and twitched as if she were having a major seizure. Her eyes rolled about and blood trickled down both nostrils. Nellie screamed and she and Claire rushed to pick up the stricken pensioner. But before they could reach her, Lily had stopped breathing. All the twitching had stopped and she lay there as dead as a dodo. Her sister, unable to believe it, kept shaking her and calling out her name. Although she was dead, the blood would not stop gushing out of the old woman's nostrils and it then also began to seep out of her ears.

At the Northern General Hospital, the doctors said it looked as if Lily had died of a brain haemorrhage. The last thing on anyone's mind was any connection between the her tragic death and the clockwork devil, waking from his slumber to cast his malevolent green gaze on its next unsuspecting victim.

George wound up the clock that night and looked closely at the word inscribed on the dial. It said, 'Fericul', supposedly the name of the French clockmaker. He thought there was something not quite right about the name but he could not think what it was.

Four days later, the devil was getting restless in his sleep again, as the clock slowly wound down, but George and Claire did not notice, as they were absorbed in a television programme. Although George was engrossed in the programme, he suddenly felt an icy chill filling the room and had the feeling he was being watched. He glanced at the clock on the mantelpiece – and saw that the devil had reawakened and was fixing them with its nasty little eyes.

As he looked at the creepy little figure, something inexplicable occurred. The little framed picture of the Pope, that Claire had reverently placed next to the clock, suddenly crashed off the mantelpiece and landed in the grate. It seemed to George that the picture had actually jumped off the mantelpiece and, naturally, it alarmed him. He did not want to scare Claire unduly, so he calmly picked up the picture, which was now cracked and said "Oh, dear!

I never did like that frame. We'll have to get a new one."

The following day, Pope Pius XII died. At first, George put it down to being just a very strange coincidence but he began to have grave suspicions about the devil on the clock. He even mentioned to Claire about his misgivings towards the diabolical figure but she said he was just being superstitious and silly.

All the same, when he returned from work, George would find himself almost continuously watching the clock, to to check whether the devil was becoming restless. Claire noticed his odd behaviour and said, "You're turning into a real clock-watcher. Stop it, will you? It's really getting on my nerves."

George decided that perhaps he was being foolish, after all, and started to watch the television and read books to pass the time, instead of gazing at the clock. Claire was probably right, he was behaving like a superstitious fool.

That Saturday, he went to the football match to watch Everton play. When he returned, he noticed that the clock was missing from the mantelpiece. Claire came into the living room and said, "Before you ask where that stupid clock is, I gave it away."

"What do you mean, 'gave it away'?" George asked. "That clock cost me twenty pounds of my hard-earned money."

"Guess what, George?" Claire said, ignoring his comments, and threw her arms around her husband.

"What?" George said, puzzled at her behaviour.

"Our Mandy and her fellah have moved into that council house in Huyton they had their eyes on. I gave her that clock for the new house. She really liked it and you said you weren't keen on it anyway."

"But ... but ..." George stammered, somehow sensing

that the clock would bring bad luck to his recently-married daughter, but not liking to say.

"But what?" Claire asked.

"Nothing," George replied, unable to put into words his serious misgivings, but he felt deeply uncomfortable about the clock being in his daughter's possession and decided to do something about it.

Without another word, he walked out of the house and asked his friend across the road to give him a lift to his daughter's new home. When he arrived at the terraced house, no one answered. He looked through the window into the living room and was filled with sheer panic at the scene which confronted him. Mandy's husband, Paul, was slumped on the sofa, and next to him, hanging halfway off the sofa, was their mongrel dog, Sam. The dog's eyes were open, yet lifeless.

George and his friend kicked the door down and entered the living room. They were greeted by a blast of stale, warm air. It was later established that Paul and the dog had died from carbon monoxide poisoning, due to a blocked flue in the gas fire. On the mantelpiece was the clock that Claire had given to the couple. The devil was sitting bolt upright, staring at Paul's dead body lying on the sofa. George's daughter suddenly came in from her trip to the shops and was surprised to see her dad and his friend. Then she saw Paul lying there next to his dog and her father sat her down and told her the terrible news. The girl dropped her shopping and let out the most pitiful wail and broke down completely.

George picked up the clock and said he was going to smash it up in the alleyway but his friend Henry stopped him and said he'd take it off his hands. A terrible thing had happened, but the idea of blaming it on a clock was just irrational. So

George, who was in a daze from the death of his son-in-law, did not put up any more resistance to the idea.

Henry would live to regret taking that clock. His family also suffered a catalogue of tragedies and mishaps, until he gradually realised that the misfortune and grief always seemed to be triggered when the devil on top of the clock awoke when the clock ran down. Rather irresponsibly, Henry sold the clock to a secondhand shop for buttons. He was glad to to see the back of the cursed thing.

By the way, no clockmaker named Monsieur Fericul has ever been traced in Rouen; but Fericul could just be an anagram of the Devil's old name.

THE ELECTRIFIED MAN

This strange incident occurred in the Broadgreen area of Liverpool and the alarming apparition mentioned in this story is still occasionally seen today.

In May 1995, an elderly couple living near the train station in Broadgreen, telephoned the police after they both sighted a man standing on the track, about six hundred yards down the line from the main platform. The couple said that the figure was "lit up", and looked as if he might be being electrocuted. The elderly man fetched his binoculars to get a better look at the figure and what he saw sent a shudder of revulsion down his spine. A man was standing on the railway track, his body racked with terrible convulsions. His mouth was wide open, with bolts of electricity shooting across his body. Smoke was billowing out of the man's mouth and from various parts of his legs and shoulders. About a minute into this horrifying spectacle, the man could no longer be seen and the electrical discharges ceased. The elderly man assumed that he had collapsed on to the track and would almost certainly be dead.

When the police converged on the track, there was no sign of any body on the line and when the videotapes of the railway security cameras were replayed, there was no footage to be found of anyone being electrocuted, or suffering a fit like the one that had been described. Yet, less than a week later, the electrified figure was reported once again, this time by passengers on a train who were disembarking at Broadgreen Station.

The witnesses told British Rail officials and the police that they had first smelt a sickening burning aroma, then had seen a man on the line, a few hundred yards away, who was illuminated by flashing blue and purple bolts of electricity that surrounded his trembling body. One of the witnesses, a student from John Moores University, let out a scream and had to look away, thinking she was witnessing a man meeting his death through electrocution. Seconds later, the travellers saw that there was no longer anybody there, just a faint wisp of smoke and the last traces of the acrid smell lingering in the air.

Two independent ghost researchers got involved in the strange case and they learned that, around the time of the sightings of the electrified man, a woman in a house overlooking the railway track, had encountered a frightening apparition in her garden at 10 o'clock one evening. She had been taking her washing off the line when her hair had suddenly stood up on end and crackled with what felt like static electricity. She also had the sensation of the hair on the back of her head being tugged.

She turned round as the static painfully tingled all over her scalp and saw a man, about twenty feet away, standing in her garden. The man was completely bald and wore bib-

and-brace type of overalls. An aura of pale blue light surrounded him and, as he walked towards her, he grinned and reached out with his arms. As he got closer, the woman felt her face begin to tingle with electricity. She dropped the washing and turned and ran as fast as she could back into her house. She slammed the door behind her and slid the bolt, before frantically telephoning her husband. A series of loud clicks came from the earpiece, so she tried to re-dial, but the same interference was on the line. Then she noticed a bluish glow near her kitchen window and there was the bald-headed figure peering in at her. She screamed, which seemed to startle the figure and it moved away.

The woman tried to telephone her husband once again and, this time, she managed to get through. He immediately returned home when he heard her story. As he drove up the drive, his car stalled for no apparent reason, as if something had interfered with the engine.

Over the rest of that month, the glowing figure was seen by a taxi driver, a newspaper delivery boy and a woman who was out walking her dog near the railway track. A psychic who became involved in the case concluded that the apparition was the ghost of a railway worker who had been electrocuted on the line in the late 1950s. He claimed that the earthbound spirit was lonely and wanted to take the life of a woman, so he would have some company.

Curiously enough, around that time, the *Liverpool Echo* also reported that there was a lot of television interference in the Broadgreen area. Was the electrified phantom the culprit?

THE CAMERA NEVER LIES

The following story is a well-documented incident which took place in the late nineteenth century in Liverpool.

In July 1897, fifty-six-year-old Mrs Eliza Marwood passed away at her home in Grove Street, Wavertree. In the front parlour of her house, she was laid to rest in an open coffin and then covered in roses. Thick white drapes on the windows, put up as a traditional mark of respect, allowed very little light into the parlour. Mr Marwood then summoned a competent photographer named Anthony Parkes to take a tasteful series of photographs of the wake but when the cameraman arrived, he pointed out that the thick curtains on the windows were not letting in sufficient light to enable him to take a photograph of the subject in the normal manner, and a flash would make the corpse seem even paler than it was.

"Then what do you propose?" asked Mr Marwood. He certainly had no intentions of opening the curtains, as that would be thought highly disrespectful.

"I will have to take a long exposure. A series of exposures, in fact, if you wish to have several plates made."

"Very well, do what you must," said Mr Marwood and the photographer replied that he would need the utmost privacy, with no interruptions. Mr Marwood left the parlour and instructed the rest of the family not to enter for an hour.

Mr Parkes was a little unnerved by the task. It was the first time he had photographed an actual corpse before, although many families who regarded the camera as a novelty were now having loved ones who had passed away photographed for posterity. He set up his camera on a tripod and, after focusing and opening the aperture to its full extent, to allow as much light into the camera as possible, he opened the shutter, uncapped the lens and stepped out of the parlour for a while. He calculated that the first exposure would require three minutes, but he did not fancy hanging around with the corpse in the silent parlour for even that short amount of time.

"Has some kind of problem arisen?" Mr Marwood asked the cameraman, who emerged from the parlour looking slightly anxious.

"No, sir," Mr Parkes reassured him, "I merely came out to minimise any vibration to the camera while it takes the photograph."

The photographer studied his pocket watch until the allotted time had passed.

Mr Parkes took two more exposures of the body and then returned to his darkroom in the attic of his house in Aigburth Road, to develop them. By the red lamp which hung from a crossbeam in the attic, he began to develop the glass plates. He held the first plate by the edges, between his fingers, and gently moved it about in the tray of developer. Very slowly, the ghostly image of Mrs Marwood started to materialise on the plate, but what Mr Parkes saw on that plate almost made him drop it with fright.

Mrs Marwood's eyes were wide open and staring with an angry, sinister look, straight into the camera lens, yet Mr Parkes had ascertained that the eyes of the corpse had been closed while it was lying in the parlour. He put the plate in the stop tray to prevent over-development, then treated it with fixer to stabilise the image.

With trepidation, he then set about developing the next plate. This picture was even more disturbing, for it showed a curious blur, which looked as though it had been caused by the corpse moving its head about during the long exposure. Mr Parkes knew this was impossible. The only explanation he could think of was that a small child had hidden in the parlour during the exposures and had moved the coffin – but that would not explain how the eyes were staring with such a life-like gaze.

The third plate was finally developed and it showed what resembled a long, fine, transparent veil, dangling vertically over the open coffin. The end of this strange cobweb-like structure seemed to taper into Mrs Marwood's mouth.

Although Mr Parkes was a scientific man, he had a sneaking suspicion that the camera had somehow captured the dead woman's spirit leaving her body. He wrestled with his principles for some time, then finally decided to show the unsettling photographs to Mr Marwood, who recoiled in terror when he saw the plates and accused the photographer of faking the strange effects with his camera. Mr Parkes pointed out that he had not even been present during the exposures; he had been standing outside the parlour as the camera recorded the strange images.

After Mr Parkes had left, a niece of Mr Marwood's came forward and revealed that something strange had happened when she had gone into the parlour to pay her last respects to her late aunt. The girl had been praying four feet away from the open coffin, when she had heard a sound. She opened her eyes and saw that three of the roses from the enormous bouquet on Mrs Marwood's chest, had just been hurled across the room and had landed on the lid of the piano. Then something even more startling happened – the niece swore that she saw her dead aunt open one eye for a moment then quickly shut it again. The girl was so scared she immediately left the parlour.

What became of the weird photographic plates is unknown, but they were meticulously analysed by the

Psychical Research Society at the time, who could provide no satisfactory explanation. However, the Marwoods' neighbours later claimed that the ghostly goings-on at the wake were due to the fact that Mr Marwood was having an affair with the very florist who had supplied him with the floral tributes for the funeral. It is said that, even today, the house in Grove Street is still haunted by the forlorn-looking phantom of the betrayed Mrs Marwood.

THE LIGHTHOUSE GHOUL

Perch Rock is a large outcrop of red sandstone which juts out into the River Mersey from the northern tip of the Wirral Peninsula. The cliffs that line the coast from Perch Rock to the Dee Estuary, are known to be riddled with tunnels and caverns that were once used by smugglers and there are many fascinating old tales about this stretch of coastline; but the following story is not about contraband, it is about murder and the supernatural ...

In the summer of 1827, the foundation stone of the New Brighton Lighthouse was laid in the middle of Perch Rock by the Liverpool Dock Trustees. Granite was brought from Anglesey and volcanic cement from the slopes of Mount Etna for the foundations of the lighthouse, which was opened in March 1830. The tower stood ninety feet high and its powerful beam was soon sweeping Liverpool Bay to guide ships on their voyages.

The first keeper, an elderly man named Garratt, died unexpectedly at the lighthouse one night and was quickly replaced by a sixty-five-year-old, ex-sea captain from Wallasey, Jack Maudley. Maudley was regarded as an odd character by those who knew him; something of a misfit. He was a loner – which, of course, made him perfect for the job – and had a black cat which he took everywhere with him. Maudley wrote to his brother in Liverpool telling him of his new job and saying that he would enjoy the isolation on Perch Rock where he would be far removed from the wagging tongues of his neighbourhood. Maudley was referring to the (not entirely unfounded) rumours of him spying on young ladies with a telescope from his attic.

Mr Maudley and his faithful feline friend soon settled in at the lighthouse. Maudley read book after book to keep himself amused and wrote several more letters to his brother. In one of these letters, he wrote that he missed his old house and even his confounded gossiping neighbours. He also mentioned that he was being tormented by strange dreams that involved making love to young women. Maudley's brother wrote back, telling him that his unhealthy, lecherous dreams could be prevented, if he would only say his prayers to the Almighty for an hour before retiring each night.

But instead, Maudley started keeping a diary, recording all his innermost and perverse thoughts. His handwriting seemed to become more jagged and angular as he wrote about his carnal cravings and, at one point in the diary, he stabbed the page repeatedly with the point of his nib.

One sunny April morning, at 11 o'clock, Maudley's heart jumped when he glanced out from the window of his quarters in the lighthouse. On the rocks below strolled a pretty girl of about seventeen or eighteen. She wore a black straw boater and was holding up her skirt to her knees, as she carefully picked her way amongst the deep pools on the rock. Under her arm was a long cane with a fine fishing net at the end and she carried a jar to hold any fish or crabs that she might catch. The girl's name was Molly Jenkins and she had ventured on to Perch Rock at low tide, the only time the rock was accessible from land. In a few hours, the tide would turn and the rock would swamped again by twenty feet of seawater.

It is hard for a normal person to imagine the intense, erotic turmoil that Maudley must have experienced, when he first set eyes upon that young maiden on that sunny morning. What vile urges the lighthouseman felt that day will never be fully known but they must have driven him to violence, because Molly Jenkins disappeared that morning, although her black straw bonnet and fishing net were found that afternoon, drifting in with the tide.

The police questioned Maudley about the missing girl and he denied having ever set eyes on her. Yet, in his secret diary, it was later discovered that the old lighthouse keeper had actually sketched a girl wearing a boater with the words, 'Molly, I am so sorry,' scrawled next to it.

On 30 July of that year, at 9 o'clock at night, Jack Maudley's sixteen-year-old nephew, Richard, came to the lighthouse carrying a lantern across Perch Rock. The tide was starting to come in and the boy began to panic. He started hammering on the main door of the lighthouse with his fist. His Uncle Jack opened the door a few minutes later and reluctantly admitted the boy into the building.

"I've run away from home, Uncle Jack," Richard told Maudley and followed him up the long winding steps to his living quarters.

"I told them I wanted to stay with you, Uncle, and my father said you ... er," the boy mumbled and could not finish the sentence.

"Your father said what?" Maudley retorted, as he halted on the steps and turned to face his nephew. His eyes narrowed, giving his face a sinister and distorted cast in the light of the lantern.

"Well, Uncle, father says you are … erm …a bit eccentric," Richard replied timidly and then blushed.

"What else did he say? Tell me!" shouted Maudley.

"He said you are always looking at girls young enough to be your granddaughters," Richard continued.

"Hah! I couldn't give a damn what people say anymore," Maudley declared and continued to ascend the stairs.

His black cat ran down to greet its master and arched its back as it spotted Richard and turned and fled up the last few steps. Richard and his uncle sat in the living quarters playing chess for a couple of hours, then the boy said he would love to see the powerful light up in the turret of the lighthouse, so Maudley took him up to have a look. The view from the turret was a vast panorama of blackness. Now and then, the revolving beam of light caused the foam of the waves below to shimmer and sparkle, but otherwise a black void encompassed the building.

At midnight, a terrible thunderstorm rolled in from the Irish Sea. Gales howled through the building and rain lashed at the windows of the turret. Lightning streaked down from the heavens and a searing, blinding bolt struck the lightning conductor on the roof with an almighty crack. Less than a heartbeat later, a powerful thunderclap shook the foundations of the lighthouse and Mr Maudley quickly escorted his nephew down to the living quarters for safety and then went back up to the turret to attend to the light.

Richard sat in front of the small open fire in the tiny room and listened to the storm raging outside. Then he heard the screams … At first, he thought it was the cat, but it soon became clear that it was a human wailing and it seemed to be coming from somewhere outside the lighthouse.

"Uncle Jack?"

Richard opened the door and crept up the steps leading

to the turret. Up in the circular room of windows, was the trembling, jibbering wreck of Jack Maudley, rocking backwards and forwards on all fours. The black cat was purring and nuzzling its affectionate little face against his arm, thinking he was playing a game. All the time, the great dazzling light in the turret turned slowly on its axis, causing Maudley's shadow to waltz crazily about the room.

"Uncle?"

Maudley jumped and turned to face him with a startled look. His face was white and his eyes bulged alarmingly.

"Go back downstairs!" the keeper shouted and then looked back at the rain-battered windows.

"What's wrong, Uncle?" Richard asked.

Then he saw all too clearly what was wrong. Something emerged from the stormy blackness. Something grotesque and hideous. It was the decomposed body of a girl. Her face was pale green and her eyes were just black sockets. Black shiny seaweed hung from her skeletal, half-naked body. The ghoul's mouth opened wide and let out the terrible wailing sound that Richard had heard moments before. Her body was lashed nearer and nearer to the windows of the turret, until the light swept over her rotting body.

Richard's stomach turned over and his knees felt weak. He was nauseous, and yet he was transfixed by the grim sight. The ghoul looked like the mortal remains of a girl he had once had a crush on – like the shell of lovely Molly Jenkins.

Jack Maudley glanced up at the screaming vision and it pointed an accusing bony finger at him. The finger tapped repeatedly on the window. Then, just as suddenly as it had started, the storm outside abated.

In the eerie calm, the corpse began to moan, "You ... It was you that killed me ..."

In blind panic, Richard fled from the glass-lined turret and ran helter-skelter downstairs in the darkness until he reached the living quarters. He seized the lantern and raced back down the winding steps to the lighthouse entrance.

A voice behind him screamed: "Richard, come back!"

"No!" Richard yelled. "You killed Molly! Father was right about you!"

The boy's heart pounded and he feared that his uncle would kill him too, now that he had discovered the horrible truth about Molly's mysterious disappearance. But when he reached the main door of the lighthouse, it was locked. Richard turned and saw his uncle's cat padding silently down the steps out of the darkness. The cat arched its back and hissed aggressively at the boy, as it bared its pointed teeth and narrowed its eyes.

Suddenly Jack Maudley loomed out of the darkness wielding a hatchet. His face had undergone a disturbing, blood-curdling transformation and bore no resemblance to the jovial fellow with whom he had been playing chess earlier in the evening.

"You shouldn't have come here tonight, Richard," snarled Maudley. "You should have stayed away from this place. Look away!" he shrieked, ready to smash the teenager's skull to pieces as quickly as possible, to prevent unnecessary suffering.

"Please don't kill me, Uncle. I won't tell, I swear I won't tell," Richard pleaded.

"I know you won't tell, laddy, because the dead can't speak," sneered Maudley, as he gritted his teeth and tapped his open palm with the blade of the hatchet, poised and ready to strike.

Richard cowered at the foot of the steps, fully expecting to meet his doom, but then something darkly comical happened. The black cat got under Maudley's feet and the keeper fell down the last ten steps of the lighthouse, gashing his forehead on the final step. The evil old mariner lay there, motionless, and richard wondered for a moment if he was dead. The hatchet fell from his hand and then Richard noticed three keys fastened with string to his uncle's belt. He pulled at them, but could not snap the strong yarn. So he removed the belt and slid off the keys. He tried the first key, but it would not open the lock, nor would the second; that was the key to Maudley's house. It had to be the third key. As Richard was fumbling to insert it into the keyhole, a strong hand snatched at his ankle.

"Come here, boy! You're not leaving here alive!" snarled Maudley. He had regained consciousness and his cat was purring with delight.

Richard let out another scream as his uncle reached for the hatchet. The lighthouse keeper seized its handle, but seemed too unsteady to stand up, instead attempting to hack at his nephew's legs from where he lay. He took an angry swipe at the boy's kneecap but Richard pulled his leg away just in time and the blade of the hatchet embedded itself deeply into the oaken door. As Maudley was trying to wrench the hatchet free, there was a pitiful moaning sound from outside.

It was the ghoul again. It was at the door.

Maudley was momentarily distracted by the awful wailing and, at that tense moment, Richard managed to turn the key and wrench open the door. As he did so, the handle of the hatchet, stuck fast in the door, rammed into Maudley's eye, almost knocking him unconscious for a second time. He let go of the boy's ankle and Richard ran screaming from the lighthouse and plunged off the rocks into the sea. As he swam frantically for the shore, choking from fear and the freezing salt water, he managed to look back just once to see the ghoul entering the lighthouse. He could not be sure, but the terrified boy thought he heard a distant shrieking sound, as he thrashed about to save himself from the waves.

At first light, two detectives and five policemen arrived at Perch Rock at low tide. They found the main door of the lighthouse standing ajar and, on the steps, they came across the body of the keeper, Jack Maudley. There were marks on the walls where Maudley had struck out at someone with his hatchet but the police were at a loss to explain just whom he had been fighting off. Stranger still, what could explain the strange rictus of death on the keeper's face? – the protruding tongue and bulging eyes which stared in terror? The detectives could see that someone had strangled the lighthouse keeper, someone with incredible, super-human strength, but why had the killer left the black, sinewy seaweed draped around Maudley's throat?

There was one solitary clue at the murder scene: a small golden charm, in the form of an anchor, which lay on the floor beside the throttled corpse. Detectives assumed that it had probably belonged to the dead man but their enquiries failed to reach a satisfactory conclusion. Maudley's black cat was the only witness to the dramatic murder.

Richard Maudley eventually told the detectives who had killed his insane uncle, but the law does not recognise the supernatural. Richard himself was suspected at first, but was cleared after a lengthy cross-examination. Through a strange quirk of fate, on the day of the terrible murder at the lighthouse, the badly decomposed body of Molly Jenkins was washed ashore on Perch Rock. The girl's mother and father came forward to identify her. Molly's father nodded in recognition but the dead girl's mother sobbed and said it could not be and the coroner asked her why not.

"She always wore her charm. A little gold anchor on a chain. I can't see any charm on this body."

The coroner shuddered when he heard this and produced the little golden anchor found at the lighthouse. Molly's mother clutched it to her lips and burst into anguished tears.

The coroner was baffled. How had the charm ended up in the lighthouse? Supposing Maudley had killed the girl, then who had strangled him? Even Maudley's warped diary, which was later discovered at the lighthouse, with its incriminating references to Molly, merely showed that the lighthouse keeper had an unbalanced mind – it didn't throw any light on the identity of the lighthouse keeper's strangler.

In the 1970s, New Brighton Lighthouse was sold off and refurbished. It was hired out to newly-married couples wanting somewhere unusual to spend their honeymoon. In 1973, one honeymooning couple allegedly heard an awful wailing sound, late one night, which seemed to come from the rock below. They did not look out of the windows, as they were too scared, but could it have been the return of the tormented ghost of Molly Jenkins – the Lighthouse Ghoul?

FORCES ARE MOVING ME

The following spate of terrifying incidents allegedly happened in the winter of 1949.

A couple and their three children moved into a crumbling old house in a street off Brownlow Hill. The couple, a Mr and Mrs Warner, had lost their home in the north end of the city, five years previously, in the Blitz. They had been moving around from one place to another in the city, until a relative told them about the four-bedroomed house which had just been vacated after the death of its solitary occupier; an old woman named Miriam Newrick.

The Warners had two beautiful twin daughters, Rita and Paula, who were fifteen years old, as well as twelve-year-old Malcolm. The family thought the old house was a considerable improvement on the dilapidated lodgings in which they had been living over the last five years and the children looked forward to having their own rooms and some measure of privacy at last.

Malcolm's mother tucked her son up into bed on the first night in his own room. She kissed his forehead and then switched out the light. That night, Malcolm had a strange dream in which he was spinning round and round in the darkness. He awoke in the pitch blackness at four in the morning, feeling dizzy and nauseous. He felt as if he wanted to be sick and got out of bed, hitting his face against the wall with a loud smack. The noise woke up the twins in their bedroom next door. They heard their brother crying and went to see what was the matter.

"What's wrong, Malcolm?" Paula asked, then screamed as she saw the blood streaming from his nose.

Malcolm had tried to get out of bed but the bed had

somehow rotated through 180 degrees. He did not realise it was facing the other way and had got up in the dark and bumped into the wall, almost breaking his nose.

When Malcolm's parents came to see what happening, they ordered the twins back to bed and told Malcolm to stop messing about, because he had school in the morning. Malcolm's dad put a handkerchief round his son's nose and when the bleeding had stopped, told him to get to sleep. Malcolm insisted that the bed had been moving around on its own but his father reminded him that it was a sin to tell lies. Malcolm finally went back to sleep and the rest of that night was uneventful.

However, on the following night, about fifteen minutes after Malcolm had got into bed, the twins heard a strange creaking noise coming from their brother's bedroom and got up to investigate. They gently opened his bedroom door and switched on the light. What they saw sent them running, terrified, to their parent's room. The bed Malcolm was sleeping on was levitating five feet above the floor and rotating at high speed, like some crazy spinning top.

When Mr and Mrs Warner came into their son's bedroom, they saw that the bed was resting in the middle of the floor and Malcolm was talking in his sleep, in a deep demonic voice. "Get out of this house, or I'll break your necks!" he cried. Then the boy woke up with a startled expression and in the same weird voice, screamed, "Mum! Forces are moving me!"

The bed started to rotate again but this time the boy was thrown out by the centrifugal force as it whizzed round. The twins ran screaming out of the bedroom and fled down the stairs, while their parents picked up their boy and looked at the spinning bed in total disbelief. A bundle of comics, belonging to Malcolm, suddenly flew at them from a bedside cabinet. Seconds later, the poltergeist activity stopped as mysteriously as it had started and the bed crashed back down to the floor.

Almost a week went by without incident then, on the following Friday night, strange whistling noises were heard coming down the chimney, as the Warners sat around the fireplace in the parlour, listening to the radio. The family huddled together, not knowing what to expect. A high-pitched voice came on the radio saying, "Hello, folks!" Then there followed a loud knocking at the door, which made the entire family jump. Mr Warner looked out of the parlour window but there was no one on the doorstep – and yet the knocker continued to bang away on the front door. The racket got so bad that eventually he grabbed the poker from the fireside and went into the hall.

"What do you want?" he demanded.

"Are those girls coming out to play?" asked a peculiar, child-like voice.

Mr Warner suspected that some local kid was playing tricks. They had probably tied a cotton thread to the knocker, or some such thing. He opened the door and looked out into the snow-covered street, then examined the knocker, which showed no sign of having been interfered with. He was looking both ways, up and down the street, when suddenly, a snowball hit him squarely in the face, almost blinding him. As he wiped the ice and snow from his eyes, he felt something brush past him. Seconds later he heard screams. He rushed into the parlour brandishing the poker and saw, to his horror, that something was pulling the twins off the floor by their pigtails. Their mother was desperately holding on to them and Malcolm was hiding under the table, crying.

As Mr Warner rushed forward, a lump of red-hot coal shot

out of the fire and narrowly missed him. The twins continued to scream and be pulled up, until their feet were dangling a couple of inches off the floor. Meanwhile, their mother was sent hurtling backwards by some invisible force, landing on the sofa. The same thing then happened to Mr Warner. The poker flew from his hand and landed in the fireplace, then something pushed him backwards, so hard that he was sent hurtling through the doorway and landed in the hall. The invisible force then let go of the twins and made a grab at Malcolm. It pulled him by his ankles from under the table and dragged him upwards so that he appeared to be doing a handstand.

Mrs Warner got in front of the hysterical twins and screamed out, "In the name of Jesus! Go away!"

A gust of ice-cold wind suddenly blew through the parlour. It was so powerful that it almost extinguished the fire in the grate. Malcolm was released and fell heavily on to his back. About an hour later, a pair of woollen gloves belonging to Mrs Warner flew around the hallway. The gloves patted the faces of the twins and one glove even shot up one of the twins' skirts. She let out a scream and the gloves darted into the fire in the parlour.

A gruff voice then spat out the words, "Spoilsports! I'll smother you all in your beds tonight!"

Enough was enough. The Warners decided there and then to move out of the wretched house. they packed their bags and set off that same night to stay with Mr Warner's brother in Aigburth.

A psychic from a spiritualist society heard about the haunting and gained permission to visit the haunted house. He said that he felt the presence of a little boy named John, who had been murdered at the house a hundred years ago. No one took the psychic's claims seriously at the time, but, twelve years later, during the demolition of the house, the skeleton of a boy was found buried beneath the cellar. The body was never identified and the cause of death was never determined with any level of certainty, but the coroner believed that a large crack over the eye socket of the boy's skull could have been the result of a violent blow inflicted while he was still alive. The coroner also estimated that the boy had died approximately one hundred years before.

OLD HAG SYNDROME

The following story has been confirmed by many sources, including testimony from the victim himself. For various reasons, the names of people and places have been changed.

In Liverpool in the early 1990s, a group of property developers bought a parcel of land that was considered a desolate eyesore. A narrow, crumbling house stood at one end of the strip of land and the landlord who owned the old dwelling enthusiastically accepted a substantial but undisclosed sum from the developers.

There were two elderly people in the house, both of them in very bad health. The old house was their home and they told the landlord that they did not want to move. The landlord warned them that a surveyor had condemned the house but, when the old people said they had not seen any surveyor, the landlord alerted the social services. Days later, the people were taken into care by two social workers and put into sheltered accommodation.

Before this happened, something seemingly amusing took place. One of the old people saw the landlord talking to one of the property developers, a forty-two-year-old man called David.

"Where's Agatha going to live now?" she shouted.

"She's not all there," the landlord whispered to the property developer behind his hand.

David then asked the old woman who Agatha was.

"Aggie!" she replied. "The same old woman who's lived with us for years. We asked her to move with us but she doesn't like the area where we're going, because there's a church right on top of us."

David did not want to make a scene and felt sorry for the old and apparently confused, woman. He knew there was nobody called Agatha at the condemned house but said, "Don't you worry, love. Agatha can stay with me if she wants."

The landlord had to turn away and his shoulders shook as he tried to stifle a chuckle.

"Are you sure?" asked the old woman and smiled as she turned to face the old house, "Aggie! This nice man here says you can move in with him."

After a long pause, the old woman said, "She accepts your invitation, as long as you don't live near a church. She's a bit eccentric about churches you see."

That really tickled the landlord.

"Aggie's eccentric?" he asked, grinning at the irony of the old woman's remark.

Something happened just then which wiped the grin off his face. The three people present heard laughter coming from the condemned house.

The property developer looked at the landlord with a puzzled expression, "Did you hear that?"

The landlord nodded and quickly added that he had to go and pick his children up from school.

And so the nightmare began. The pensioner went off to say goodbye to her old friends who lived around the corner and the developer fastened his seatbelt and drove off, feeling suddenly quite uneasy. He drove to his luxurious home in Maghull and, as he got out of his Mercedes, he distinctly felt someone pat his bottom. He glanced around but there was no one about.

David told his wife Emma about the weird laughter in the house but she said he was being silly. They had dinner that evening and then Emma went to visit her friend, Kay, who lived some miles away in Downholland Cross. Kay was involved in the preparations for a relative's wedding and Emma had promised to help out.

So David was left alone for three hours that evening; or at least he thought he was alone. He put on a classical record, opened a bottle of wine and relaxed on his Chesterfield sette, lost in Mozart. Half an hour later, he had fallen asleep.

Some time later, he was woken by something pressing down painfully on his chest. At first he thought that Emma had returned and was playing about, but when he opened his eyes, he discovered that a hideous old woman with a long hooked nose was pinning him down. He couldn't move. He was totally paralysed. He tried to speak but could only touch the roof of his mouth with his tongue, which felt dead. The old hag smiled to reveal three decaying yellowed teeth and saliva oozed from both ends of her sickly, sagging pink lips. Her face was a mass of deep wrinkles and flabby jowls. Her watery eyes were yellow and red veins encircled her faded bluish-grey irises. She looked as if she was centuries old. Her claw-like hands reached up and undid a bun of greasy white locks, which tumbled down past her shoulder.

In a vile and raspy voice she cackled, "You're a fine lad and no mistake!"

David's heart felt as if it was going to explode. He kept trying to wake up from the nightmare but it slowly dawned on him that this was no dream, it was really happening. The old crone licked his lips with her pink tongue, which was mottled with white warts.

"Ooh, I'll stay with you as your wife, if you desire, eh?"

David closed his eyes firmly for a few seconds then reopened them in the hope that she would have disappeared. The old hag was still there, still trying to molest him. From somewhere deep down, David managed to summon up the strength to move. He cried out from the bottom of his lungs and the old woman screamed back in protest. He somehow managed to lift his arm and he took a swipe at the gruesome figure but it felt as if he was hitting a sack of bones. Suddenly she was gone.

David staggered to his feet and saw, to his horror, that the shadowy figure of the old woman was now at the other end of the lounge. She wet her fingers and began pinching the wicks of the perfumed candles, extinguishing them, one by one. He turned up the light dimmer and was able to see the weird-looking old woman in full light for the first time. She was bent and crooked and she grinned at him – then disappeared.

He jumped into his Mercedes and drove frantically to his friend, Alec's house, about three miles away. Throughout the journey, the property developer continually felt something stroking his hair.

When David told Alec about being terrorised by the old hag, his friend assumed that the wine had gone to his head, but David convinced him that he was sober and deadly serious. Alec asked him why the ghost of an old woman would choose to pester him and David suddenly remembered the old woman who was being forced to move from the condemned house and her concern for Agatha, whoever she might be. Now it all began to make sense. Tongue-in-cheek, David had jokingly suggested that Agatha could move in with him.

"It is a bit of a coincidence, I suppose," admitted Alec, when he heard about the incident.

"Please believe me, Alec. That thing is demonic. How the heck do I get rid of her?" said David earnestly.

"I don't know. Tell her to pack her bags."

"How do you mean?"

"Just tell her to beat it."

David sighed and shook his head saying, "I don't think it's going to be as easy as that. But hang on a minute," he continued, "that woman today; she said something about Aggie not liking churches."

"I think you're having me on," Alec laughed nervously.

But David was definitely not laughing. "Alec, have you got a Bible?"

"Look, don't you think you're taking this a bit too seriously, David," Alec said, becoming increasingly disturbed by his friend's behaviour.

"Please, I'm asking you, have you got a Bible?" David repeated and he scanned the large mahogany bookcase behind his friend.

"Okay yes, not that I ever read it. Here you are."

Alec pulled a large leather-bound copy of the Bible from the shelf.

"I hope to God this works. I'll ring you later," David said and left.

Returning home, David sat in his lounge, watching the television. Suddenly, he saw something move out the corner of his eye. He turned and saw the old hag cowering in the corner of the room. Emma was due back any minute, so he had to act now.

"Why don't you come here?" he asked the frightful apparition.

"Throw that blasted book away and I will!" hissed the old woman.

"Are you Agatha?" David asked, picking up the Bible.

"Yes. Please be rid of that book, m'dear. Go on, throw it on the fire," urged Agatha, staring at the Bible as if it were the most loathsome object.

"You're not wanted in here any more. Get out of this house," said David, plucking up enough courage to take the book over to Agatha.

"You don't mean it! I know you enjoyed my caresses," leered the withered old crone.

"In the name of God, I order you to leave my home," said David, gaining in confidence as the woman cringed before him. It was then that he noticed that she was also becoming more transparent.

"I thought you loved me," Agatha went on, her voice becoming fainter.

He hurled the Bible at the grotesque vision and it vanished before the book could pass through it.

David never told Emma about his supernatural ordeal but his wife was perplexed when he came home the next day with five copies of the Bible. The property developer placed the holy books in different rooms of the house and later visited the two old people he had forced into sheltered accommodation. He asked them who Agatha was, but they refused to comment. The old woman just said, "So you met her then?" and smiled, knowingly.

David has not set eyes on the old hag since that day, but he had graphic nightmares about her for over a year.

According to psychologists and psychical researchers, David's case is by no means an isolated one. For centuries, many people (mostly males) have reported being terrorised and assaulted by sinister entities like the witch that molested David. In fact, many psychologists have named the bizarre phenomenon, 'Old Hag Syndrome' and have noted that the traumatic experience of being assaulted seems utterly real to the victim and usually occurs shortly before sleep, or just after the sleeper has awoken in the middle of the night. Involuntary catatonia (a sudden onset of paralysis) has been blamed but this does not explain why the victim sees and feels the presence of a hideous crone during the episodes. Furthermore, Old Hag Syndrome is apparently on the increase ... sweet dreams!

THE RETURNED MAN

This is a bizarre story, yet it was witnessed by nine people in broad daylight in the middle of Liverpool in the 1960s. The incident was investigated by Dr Ivan Hunter, the late Cambridge professor of psychology who systematically studied alleged mediums and psychics.

The story unfolded in 1968, when a couple in their forties were leaving the Swan Pub in Liverpool's Wood Street. As Joan and Frank walked up the street, Frank told his wife he loved her, then fell down dead in the road from a massive coronary. Joan sat in the road cradling her husband, sobbing, surrounded by bystanders. An ambulance turned up but the medics could not help; Frank was dead and they could do nothing to bring him back.

After the funeral, Joan went into a terrible depression that seemed to have no end. Every evening, for over six months, she walked aimlessly around Kirkby, dressed in black, with her head bowed. She visited all the places she used to go to with her late husband; the bingo, the Peacock pub, the park where they strolled hand in hand in the summer. She even went to look at the old bus shelter where she had first told Frank that she was pregnant.

One bright summer morning, Joan's four sons and their wives and girlfriends turned up at her home with flowers, chocolates and gifts to cheer their mother up. They persuaded her to go to town to do some shopping with them. Reluctantly, Joan got ready and one of her sons, Michael, drove her to town, followed by the others. All was going well, until Joan spotted a young couple in Church Street, who looked exactly like a young version of herself and her late husband. The couple were walking along, hand in hand, smiling at each other. Joan dropped the bag and started to cry. Her sons surrounded her and comforted her.

Joan broke down, "I can't go on without him. They say it gets better as time goes on, but I can't take it any more. I wish I was with him, I really do." A bald, distinguished-looking man, wearing sunglasses, came forward. He was dressed in a finely-cut dark blue suit and spoke in a reassuring voice. "Excuse me," he said to Joan's sons and moved through them and their wives until he reached the bewildered Joan. The stranger put his arm around Joan's shoulder and produced a neatly folded handkerchief. "Here, have a good blow," he said and, turning to her sons added, "Look, I know your mother. Can I just talk to her in private for a moment?" He then took Joan over to a jeweller's window and said, "Look, Joan, Frank is beside himself with grief because of the way you're behaving. You're like a little child."

Joan was confused by the his words: "What? Are you some sort of psychic?"

The man smiled, "If you knew what I was, you'd run a mile. Now, if I could convince you that Frank is okay, would you promise not to go on crying all the time and being a downright misery?"

Joan nodded, wondering if the man was some religious crank or a confidence trickster.

"You haven't said you'd promise," continued the man.

"I promise," Joan sobbed, wiping away her tears.

The man then pointed towards a tailor's shop, near the corner of Whitechapel and Church Street. There stood Frank as large as life. He nodded, smiling at Joan and laughing in reaction to the way his wife's jaw dropped.

"Frank! Frank!" shouted Joan and thrust her arms out towards the familiar figure at the end of the street.

As she started to walk towards him, the stranger held her back, saying, "You can't, Joan."

By now, one of Joan's sons, Michael, had also seen the vision of his father on the corner and Frank waved to him and gave him the thumbs up. Michael was understandably shocked and told his brothers and his wife to look and they too saw the figure. Michael shouted, "Dad!" and fought through the crowds to get to him but when he reached the corner, Frank was nowhere to be seen. His brothers, their wives and girlfriends following behind, were all in a state of total confusion. When they returned to Joan, she was alone, the stranger had left.

From that day onwards, Joan started to rebuild her life and stopped wearing black. She changed into an outgoing woman overnight and told her sons that she now knew that Frank was still around. She felt as if he was literally just around some corner and that there was nothing to grieve over.

Professor Hunter interviewed all the witnesses at length and concluded that they had collectively hallucinated an apparition of Frank but he admitted there was something strange about the case. The professor sought out the jeweller in the street where the incident had happened and he said that he remembered the man in the blue suit who had comforted Joan, although he had never seen him before and had not seen him since. Joan went on record as saying that she thought the man in the blue suit was some sort of angel sent by a higher authority to give her hope. The whole case remains baffling and Joan herself has since died. Perhaps she is with Frank now, wherever that might be.

THE MYSTERIOUS MR MOORE

The son of a man who worked as a porter at The Bee Hotel, which used to stand in Queen's Square in the centre of Liverpool, passed a strange story on to me that his father had often told him. The tale concerned one of the regular guests, the remarkable George Moore, who had stayed at the hotel during the 1930s. This guest had a sinister knack of foretelling tragedy, or major world events, and could allegedly even accurately predict how long a person was going to live.

On 26 June 1936, everyone, guests and staff alike, rushed out of the hotel and looked skywards at the looming mass of the *Hindenberg* – Germany's giant Zeppelin, which was returning from New York, homeward-bound for Hamburg. As the magnificent airship glided eerily over the city, one of the guests remarked that he would love to fly in the Zeppelin. Mr Moore looked at him rather scathingly, and shaking his head said, "That ship will go down in flames. Mark my words!"

Exactly one year later, the *Hindenberg*, the body of which

was filled with inflammable hydrogen gas, exploded like a bomb in mid-air. It turned into a gigantic fireball which floated down in the skies over Lakehurst, near Boston, killing all thirty-six people on board. Pictures of its demise were sent around the world and became seared on people's memories, rather like the 9/11 images which filled our television screens when New York's twin towers were deliberately destroyed by hijacked terrorist planes.

When an American guest booked into the hotel just before the outbreak of the Second World War, Mr Moore approached him and began to lecture him on his country's foreign policy, saying that America should be ashamed for sitting on the fence in the impending conflict. The American was rather taken aback by this unexpected attack on his country and bristling with indignation, he rose to its defence, claiming that it was Europe's war, why should they get involved?

"You might see things a little differently when Pearl Harbour gets hit," retorted Mr Moore.

The American had not even heard of Pearl Harbour at that time, and nor had most people – until Japan attacked it, two years later, in 1941, decimating the American fleet. Only then did he recall Moore's chilling prediction.

Moore also predicted the Apollo moon landings and the building of the Channel Tunnel, well before either project had even been conceived, never mind reached the planning stage. He also made one other very important prediction that has not, as yet, come to pass – that the British Monarchy would be ousted by four foreign men from a political party with a circle of stars as its symbol. Sound familiar?

His foresight was truly wide-ranging and he was able to predict social trends, as well as political world events. For example, he prophesied that a generation would come that would dance to the beat of a machine and choose pleasure pills in place of alcohol in their leisure time. Surely he was referring to members of the techno-rave generation, who have largely dispensed with traditional leisure drinking and opted for designer drugs like Ecstasy instead?

DON'T LOOK UNDER THE BED

This story took place in 1965 and was related to me by the two people featured in the tale, Muriel and Kenny, who now live in Wallasey. If you're reading this story in bed – don't have nightmares!

At 1.30 in the morning, Muriel and Kenny left the Mardi Gras nightclub in Mount Pleasant. They were both in their early twenties and deeply in love. The only trouble was that Kenny's parents hated Muriel's parents and vice versa, so the couple had moved out of their homes in Kensington to live together in a boarding house off Liverpool's Oxford Street. They arrived there at about ten to two and had to sneak up to their bedsit so as not wake up Hilda, their elderly landlady. Once in their room, Muriel got into bed and Kenny put the kettle on the one-ring gas stove to make a cup of tea. Muriel lit up a cigarette and relaxed in the old but sturdy double bed. Kenny made the tea, then said he had to go the toilet, so he crept out the room and sneaked down to the outside loo, which was situated in the back yard. Muriel, meanwhile, was thinking about the great night she had just had. She worked in John Collier's department store and would be getting her wage packet tomorrow and that meant another great night out with Kenny at the Basement Club, or Reeces Ballroom.

As she puffed on her cigarette, she was startled by a

strange sound in the room. The noise sounded asthmatic – like a cough. Suddenly, she heard someone, or something, make a hooting sound, like someone saying, "Ooh".

Muriel prayed for Kenny to hurry back and in the tense silence, she clearly heard a quivering voice say, "Oh, Mother of God, no!" That was enough. She jumped off the bed as if it was on fire and ran out of the room, almost falling head first down the stairs in blind panic. She met Kenny coming up and told him about the voice in their room.

"Don't be soft, Muriel. It's the landlady talking in her sleep. These walls are paper-thin. Come on, I'm dead beat."

"But it sounded as if it was … as if it was …" Muriel could not finish the sentence.

"Sounded as if it was what?" Kenny asked.

"Nothing," replied Muriel, as she climbed the stairs, clutching Kenny's hand.

"Go on," said Kenny, "it sounded as if it was what?"

Muriel squeezed Kenny's hand tightly, "It sounded as if it was under the bed."

Just then a voice behind them shouted, "Oi!"

Muriel and Kenny jumped with fright but it was only Hilda, wearing a funny-looking hairnet and a long gold lamé nightgown. She had bloodshot eyes and looked furious.

"Do you two know it's gone two o'clock in the morning? The bloomin' bolt's going on at twelve o'clock next time, I'm telling you!" she snapped and disappeared back into her bedroom, slamming the door.

Kenny and Muriel grinned at each other and went back to their room.

"She looked like Joan Crawford in that nightgown," Kenny joked, and Muriel had to stifle a laugh.

They had a cup of tea, went to bed and fell fast asleep.

At four in the morning, something awakened Muriel. It

was a faint, creepy, whispering voice, like someone saying a prayer, followed by the faint sounds of sobbing. Muriel's heart fluttered with fear and she shook Kenny awake. He heard the sound too and sat up in bed. Suddenly, something thumped the underside of the mattress.

With a dry throat, Muriel whispered, "It's under the bed, Kenny."

"Don't be soft, Muriel. It sounds like someone's got a radio on in the distance somewhere."

Then he, too, felt the thump underneath him. He was more intrigued than scared and reached out for his cigarette lighter and flicked it on. He got out of bed, bent down, looked under the bed and jokingly said, "There's a bogeyman here."

Then Kenny let out a scream. He ran out the room and dropped the lighter, leaving Muriel in the pitch-black bedsit. Muriel, terrified, got out of bed and searched frantically for the door.

Then she heard a voice crying, "no! No! Please don't hurt me!"

Almost fainting with fear, she found the door at last and ran down the stairs. At the bottom, she fell over Kenny, who had fallen down the last two steps and was lying there, dazed. Hilda came out and switched on the landing light. She was absolutely furious and promised her noisy lodgers that they would be evicted in the morning but Kenny and Muriel left the lodging house 15 minutes later and stayed in Muriel's aunt's place in Arundel Avenue. Kenny said he had seen an old woman covered in blood with staring eyes under the bed.

A month later, in the Pink Parrot Club, a Merchant Navy seaman who had once stayed in the Oxford Street lodging house, several years back, told Kenny and Muriel the story behind the haunted bed. He said that, at the turn of the century, an escaped convict from Kirkdale Gaol had broken into an old woman's house in Aigburth and had stabbed her to death as she lay hiding under her bed. The murderer then escaped with her savings and was never caught. The niece of the old woman was Hilda, the landlady of the Oxford Street lodging house and she inherited the bed. Many people, over the years, had sworn that they had heard the old woman's final pleas being whispered under that bed, but Hilda was too mean to get rid of it.

In 1969, Hilda, the landlady, died and the whispering bed was sold to a certain second-hand furniture store in Liverpool. Could it be the very same bed you are sleeping in tonight?

HARASSMENT IN THE WORKPLACE

In 1990, a firm of Liverpool solicitors kept having trouble with their alarm system. Every night, the alarm would go off and one of the partners would have to go to the premises and investigate. Invariably it would prove to be a false alarm (pardon the pun!) and it was becoming very tiresome. The alarm engineer, who was repeatedly called out, could not find any fault in the system and was at a loss as to what to do next.

Shortly afterwards, the office fax machines started switching on and off for no apparent reason and, at the same time, the secretaries started getting nuisance phonecalls from a man calling himself Roy. He told one secretary that he used to work in the building where the solicitors were sited and would giggle salaciously as he accurately described what she was wearing, right down to the type and colour of underwear she had on. The calls were finally traced to an old number in the empty room above the solicitors' office. Yet there was no phone in that room anymore and none had been connected for over twenty years.

The calls stopped for a while and the atmosphere in the office was gradually becoming much more relaxed, until one afternoon when a secretary was working at her word processor, when she suddenly felt the temperature in the room drop dramatically. Then something brushed past her back and she naturally jumped and looked about, but there was no one there. Then, as she stood up to take a better look, invisible fingers pinched her bottom!

The secretary let out a scream and ran out of her office and into her boss's. He calmed her down and then accompanied her back to her own office. As they walked in they saw that the word processor was busy typing – all by itself! Not only that, but the actual words being typed on the screen were of a very personal nature and made the boss cringe with embarrassment. The ghost was typing out little intimate snippets about the boss's extra-marital affairs; details which nobody, other than himself and his mistresses, could possibly have known. As the boss and his secretary looked on in stunned silence, the ghost signed himself off with the line, "Roy knows!"

At this point, the solicitors decided that they needed professional help to rid the office of this Roy character's unwanted and creepy attentions, or they were in danger of losing half their staff. Two psychics were called in and they held a seance at the haunted office, after the staff had gone home for the night. They both reported back that they had strongly felt the presence of the spirit of a man who had died in the 1930s – a man by the name of Roy Sykes!

Research revealed that Roy had been a clerk – and also something of a sex pest – at an office in the building now occupied by the solicitors. The circumstances of his death are unknown.

The ghostly goings-on at the office gradually faded, and an uneasy peace was restored, but the alarm system still malfunctions from time to time for no apparent reason. Could it be that raunchy Roy is still playing his dirty tricks?

THE PHILADELPHIA EXPERIMENT

Most people who are interested in mysteries, UFOs etc, will have heard of the so-called Philadelphia Experiment. The story began circulating in America, in 1956, that an alleged top-secret experiment had been conducted by the US Navy in October 1943, in which a ship, an escort destroyer, the *USS Eldridge*, was somehow rendered invisible using an electronic form of camouflage. A number of witnesses involved in the early electronic stealth project, have come forward over the years. One of them, US Marine, Carlos Allende, said that Einstein and a number of American and British scientists, had developed a type of generator which produced very intense magnetic fields. These fields could bend and polarise light rays in such a way as to make anything within the field transparent, or partially invisible. The idea being, that if Britain and America could make their destroyers and Atlantic convoys invisible to the naked eye and undetectable to radar, it would obviously be of enormous military advantage.

The magnetic generator was fitted onto the *USS Eldridge*, while it was berthed at the docks in Philadelphia. Gigawatts of electricity were pumped into the generator and the result was astounding. The air started to turn dark around the ship, then a foggy green mist rose up around it. The ship gradually faded away, until it could not be seen at all by the human eye. About a minute later, the destroyer briefly reappeared as a shimmering silvery mirage, like the ones you often see at the end of a road surface on a hot day.

One of the sailors on the waterfront described how he reached out and shoved his arm into the force field, right up to the elbow. His arm vanished and he could see a cross-section of the bone and blood vessels in his forearm, where the magnetic field ended. When the sailor stepped forward into the field, he could just make out the ghostly figures of the destroyer's crew, but he was unable to see the ship on which they were standing, so it looked as if they were suspended in mid air. Minutes afterwards, the power was shut off and the *USS Eldridge* reappeared. Initially, the experiment seemed like a success, but disturbing side effects were later suffered by most of the crew members.

A few days later, two of the men from the destroyer were in a dockside bar, when they vanished in full view of all the drinkers in the packed room. They never reappeared! Then three other crew members burst into flames and continued to burn for over eighteen days, because nothing could put out the flames; even sand melted into a glassy substance, when it was dumped on the bodies. Other crew members became paralysed and as rigid as statues, then died because they could not breathe. Researchers interested in the experiment have delved into the Navy records for years but most of the archives referring to the *USS Eldridge* have been altered or deleted.

One dark stormy morning in November 1943, a curious incident was reported closer to home, but was censored by the War Office. Fishermen in southern Ireland, near Cork Harbour, saw something very bizarre moving through St George's Channel during a thunderstorm. At first they thought it was a U Boat, but it was much more unusual. A ship's hull could clearly be detected in the water, but there was no ship there. Then, suddenly, a bolt of lightning hit the object and, for a brief instant, the fishermen saw the illuminated image of a large convoy ship. Whatever that thing was, it interfered with the fishermen's radio sets and deflected their compasses. The ship moved off and the fishermen heard its engines, but assumed that there was something supernatural about it.

All convoys on that route were bound for Liverpool Docks so, is there a connection with the Philadelphia Experiment and the Battle of the Atlantic Headquarters in Liverpool? I wonder if anyone working on the docks in 1943 saw anything strange, or heard any rumours about the invisible Atlantic conveyer?

THE MYSTERIOUS NUN

In 1964, sixty-year-old Everton man, Patrick O'Rourke, was working for Martindales, a coal merchant. He was humping a heavy bag of coal up several flights of steps to the fourth landing of a tenement block off Brownlow Hill, the Bullring Tenements to be precise, when he suddenly felt overwhelmingly dizzy. He collapsed on the stairs, where one of the residents, a Mrs Scott, found him lying semi-conscious, clutching a medal of the Blessed Virgin Mary. The other coalmen rushed up to the landing and carried him down to the coal-lorry and then quickly drove him to the Royal Liverpool Hospital.

He had suffered a severe stroke and things looked extremely bleak. Mrs O'Rourke and her family crowded into the ward where her husband lay dying. Surrounding his bed, they all prayed fervently for his recovery. Dr Bosankay, who had been treating him, advised his distressed wife to go home that night, as there was nothing she could do at the hospital. But she begged the doctor to allow her and her eldest daughter to stay, which he reluctantly allowed.

At 3am that morning, Patrick O'Rourke's breathing became shallow and laboured and then ceased altogether; his wife and daughter began to sob hysterically as his life ebbed away. In deep emotional turmoil, they were suddenly startled as an unfamiliar nun entered the room unannounced. "Don't cry," she calmly urged them, before silently gliding round the side of the bed and reached out and clutched Mr O'Rourke's hand.

"Thank you, sister," Mrs O'Rourke stammered, choking back the tears.

She felt desperately sad and hugged her daughter, but they both felt comforted by the presence of the reassuring nun. It was at that moment that Mr O'Rourke suddenly opened his eyes. He looked first at the nun's kindly face and then at his wife and daughter. "What are you crying for?" he innocently asked, before complaining of a terrible thirst. His wife and daughter flung their arms about his neck and smothered him with kisses. Then, overwhelmed with joy, they turned to thank the nun, whom they were convinced was somehow responsible for his miraculous recovery, only to find that the ward was now empty. Mrs O'Rourke could not contain herself and felt the urge to tell someone about the kindly nun who had seemingly brought her husband back from the brink of death. She began to tell an old man who been woken by the commotion about the miraculous events which had just taken place and about the nun's involvement in his recovery.

"She's a ghost," said the old man, interrupting her.

He explained that the nun had been seen on other occasions in the Royal Liverpool and other local hospitals. Apparently she was well known amongst the patients and sometimes gave her name as Veronica. Mrs O'Rourke was intrigued and later that week she spoke about the mysterious nun to Dr Bosankay. At the mere mention of the nun's involvement he turned pale. He seemed lost for words, and said that no nuns worked in the hospital, especially at three o'clock in the morning. He nevertheless admitted that he and his colleagues were completely baffled by Patrick O'Rourke's amazing recovery. Even after keeping him in for observation, he simply could not explain his sudden and total recovery.

That same week, Mrs O'Rourke told her parish priest about the strange incident. He did not seem to be at all alarmed by the claim and revealed that a nun had also recently appeared to a child in the Children's Hospital in Myrtle Street. That child had miraculously recovered from life-threatening meningitis overnight. Apparently, the nun had also been seen by a night nurse who had heard the angelic-looking woman actually identify herself as Sister Veronica. There were rumours that the same phantom nun had been encountered at the Notre Dame Convent in Hope Street, many years before.

In 1965, a mysterious nun also appeared at a house in Bromborough, where a Mrs Durban was giving birth. After a long and difficult labour, a healthy baby girl was finally born. However, the mother faded rapidly after the delivery and then lost consciousness. The midwife was seriously concerned and rushed to telephone for an ambulance. When she returned to the bedroom, she found a willowy nun leaning over Mrs Durban. An anxious-looking Mr Durban was holding his wife's hand, repeatedly whispering, "There's no pulse".

The midwife was mystified by the nun's sudden appearance and asked her how she had got into the house, but received no reply. The nun just silently put the palms of her hands on each side of Mrs Durban's face and started to whisper a melodious prayer. Mr Durban later reported that he distinctly remembered the nun uttering something about Saint Anthony.

About a minute later, Mr Durban felt a weak fluttering in his wife's wrist – her pulse had returned! As he hugged her tightly she faintly murmured the words, "I want to come back to see my baby". Her husband then became slightly alarmed, because at that moment, the nun's face had seemed to radiate a startling golden light.

Mrs Durban regained full consciousness in a cold, clammy sweat, still in the comforting embrace of her husband. The ambulance arrived at that moment and, in the confusion, no one saw the obscure nun leave. The ambulance-men stated that they had seen no one pass them on the path outside, even though that was the only way the nun could have left the premises. So, was the ethereal nun actually a ghost and could she have been the mysterious Veronica?

If you have had a paranormal encounter, or a supernatural
experience of any sort, please drop a line to
Tom Slemen c/o the address below.

THE BLUECOAT PRESS
3 Brick Street
Liverpool L1 0BL

Telephone 0151 707 2390
Website www.bluecoatpress.co.uk